ROUTLEDGE LIBRARY EDITIONS: LIBRARY AND INFORMATION SCIENCE

Volume 39

FINANCIAL PLANNING FOR LIBRARIES

FINANCIAL PLANNING FOR LIBRARIES

Edited by
MURRAY S. MARTIN

LONDON AND NEW YORK

First published in 1983 by The Haworth Press, Inc.

This edition first published in 2020
by Routledge
2 Park Square, Milton Park, Abingdon, Oxon OX14 4RN

and by Routledge
52 Vanderbilt Avenue, New York, NY 10017

Routledge is an imprint of the Taylor & Francis Group, an informa business

© 1983 The Haworth Press, Inc.

All rights reserved. No part of this book may be reprinted or reproduced or utilised in any form or by any electronic, mechanical, or other means, now known or hereafter invented, including photocopying and recording, or in any information storage or retrieval system, without permission in writing from the publishers.

Trademark notice: Product or corporate names may be trademarks or registered trademarks, and are used only for identification and explanation without intent to infringe.

British Library Cataloguing in Publication Data
A catalogue record for this book is available from the British Library

ISBN: 978-0-367-34616-4 (Set)
ISBN: 978-0-429-34352-0 (Set) (ebk)
ISBN: 978-0-367-37129-6 (Volume 39) (hbk)
ISBN: 978-0-367-37132-6 (Volume 39) (pbk)
ISBN: 978-0-429-35278-2 (Volume 39) (ebk)

Publisher's Note
The publisher has gone to great lengths to ensure the quality of this reprint but points out that some imperfections in the original copies may be apparent.

Disclaimer
The publisher has made every effort to trace copyright holders and would welcome correspondence from those they have been unable to trace.

Financial Planning for Libraries

Murray S. Martin, Editor

The Haworth Press
New York

Financial Planning for Libraries has also been published as *Journal of Library Administration*, Volume 3, Numbers 3/4, Fall/Winter 1982.

Copyright © 1983 by The Haworth Press, Inc. All rights reserved. Copies of articles in this publication may be reproduced noncommercially for the purpose of educational or scientific advancement. Otherwise, no part of this work may be reproduced or utilized in any form or by any means, electronic or mechanical including photocopying, microfilm and recording, or by any information storage and retrieval system without permission in writing from the publisher. Printed in the United States of America.

The Haworth Press, Inc., 28 East 22 Street, New York, NY 10010

Library of Congress Cataloging in Publication Data
Main entry under title:

Financial planning for libraries.

   Previously published in Journal of library administration, v. 3, no. 3-4.
   Includes bibliographical references.
   1. Library finance. 2. Library administration.
I. Martin, Murray S.
Z683.F49   1983   025.1'1   82-23346
ISBN 0-86656-118-8

Financial Planning for Libraries

Journal of Library Administration
Volume 3, Numbers 3/4

CONTENTS

FROM THE EDITOR   1

Financial Planning: Introductory Thoughts   3
   Murray S. Martin

PART I: GENERAL FINANCIAL PRINCIPLES

Issues in the Financial Management of Research Libraries   13
   Duane E. Webster

      In facing a period of financial stringency librarians need to be more creative in their approach. Two strategies are required, one external, one internal. Externally, libraries need to seek new allies in the computer center, industry and the information industry, and develop a deeper understanding of the true role and strength of the library within the institution. Internally, closer attention needs to be given to costs, functional organization, creative financing and better internal controls.

Financial Planning Needs of Publicly-Supported Academic
Libraries in the 1980s: Politics as Usual   23
   Edward R. Johnson

      A survey of fifty-five libraries at doctorate-granting Universities was conducted to determine their expectations of the future and their possible responses. A large majority foresaw insufficient resources. The chief library problems related to the costs of materials and equipment while University attention was primarily directed to research and automation, the latter also being expected to affect library budgets. Greater understanding of the library's role on campus is seen as a prerequisite for improved funding.

Planning and Finance: A Strategic Level Model
of the University Library   37
   Jerome Yavarkovsky

      This essay describes a strategic level model of the university library to support library-wide forecasting, budgeting and program cost accounting. The model is a two-dimensional array of financial elements and service programs supported by descriptive sub-models. In one dimension it displays expenditure and income relationships. In a second, it displays the relationship of financial variables to service programs. Expense and income relationships can be manipulated to reflect current operations or project anticipated levels of activity. The success of translating the array of figures into a useful tool depends on the quality of program definitions and financial variable identification.

Academic Library Decision Support Systems 55
Michael Bommer
Ronald Chorba

The growth of electronic information systems has increased the library's difficulties in providing access to that knowledge, but it has also increased the librarian's ability to control and manage the library. In order to do that effectively, however, the librarian must develop greater decision-making skills. This paper proposes the development of an electronic decision support system, which can use the information generated in the library and the parent institution and yet be adaptable to the style of the library manager.

Returning to the Unified Theory of Budgeting: An Umbrella Concept for Public Libraries 73
Harold R. Jenkins

This paper highlights essential management attitudes, operational principles and budgetary strategies that should undergird the budgeting of successful programs for all public libraries, large, medium and small.

PART II: ISSUES IN SPECIFIC BUDGET CATEGORIES

Salary Planning 87
Paul M. Gherman

Salary planning proposes that even within the context of the parent institution effective salary planning and budgetary control can take place. First, a systematic program of personnel administration, including task analysis, job design, classification, performance evaluation, and staff development should be set up so that the work of the organization can be appropriately measured and compensation just and equitable. Second, long-range planning for personnel needs must take into account the developmental costs associated with the changing nature of libraries. Algorithms must be developed to project the costs associated with the effects of automation on publishing, bibliographic networks, and library operations.

Interlibrary Loan and Resource Sharing: New Approaches 99
Noelene P. Martin

The introduction of computer-based technology has revolutionized interlibrary loan. Fast access to bibliographic information and rapidly developing electronic communication systems now enable Interlibrary Loan to function as an integral component of any collection development plan. Libraries need to rethink the organizational, functional and financial status of Interlibrary Loan to take full advantage of this new capability.

Financial Planning for Collection Management   109
   Frederick C. Lynden

> *In preparing and justifying any request for financial support for the acquisition of materials librarians must take into account financial, economic, political, environmental, and education factors. Not only must these factors be understood, they must be explained to faculty and administration. In particular the close relationship between library collections and academic goals should be stressed. More precision in defining collection goals is needed and more attention to resource sharing.*

Budgeting for and Controlling the Cost of *Other* in Library
   Expenditures: The Distant Relative in the Budgetary Process   121
   Sherman Hayes

> *The third category in library budgets tends simply to be an aggregation of all other expenditures, i.e., other than personnel and library materials. It usually represents 10-20% of the whole budget but it covers a wide range of types of expenditure, each of which may require a different approach. With the advent of computerization, this category will increase in size and importance and library managers should pay much more attention to it.*

FROM THE EDITOR

As one should expect, it is impossible to plan without consideration of financial implications. It is likewise impossible to reflect on financial planning without integrating it into all planning. It is safe to say that nothing is free, whether we are talking about dollars or other costs associated with providing a product or service. In this day and age, financial considerations weave themselves heavily into the deliberations and actions of administrators. In many cases, money may even dominate as a trigger to action or as a key criterion in decision making. Our present financial situation, despite the difficulties it creates, has fortunately served as a catalyst to initiate or rejuvenate planning activities. Desirable side effects may follow: more skill and appreciation brought to the planning process, more motivation to plan regularly, and better use of the resources we do have.

This second special issue of *JLA* is on the topic of financial planning. It is an important and solid contribution to library administration and a helpful, natural addition to our initial special edition on planning which was guest edited by Charles McClure for Volume 2 in 1981. Murray S. Martin, guest editor for this edition, has brought together a set of papers that are needed and should be well received by library administrators and students in librarianship and information services. Guest editors work very hard and deserve our attention. Murray Martin, in designing, organizing and refining this work has ably pulled together the talents of the contributing authors. They all have given considerable thought and effort to their topics, and cover a wide range of financial issues.

JLA would like to express its appreciation to Murray Martin and to his contributing authors. We hope that you will find their work both illuminating and useful, not only in what they say but in the additional citations they provide for your use. It is hoped that their efforts will stimulate improved planning and use of financial resources, and ultimately serve the public in improved ways.

John R. Rizzo

Financial Planning: Introductory Thoughts

Murray S. Martin

No matter how much money is available some planning must accompany its expenditure if the resultant benefits are in any way to match the expectations of those who provide the money. When there is less money the setting of plans for its expenditure is even more critical. For many years in the 60s and early 70s the supply of money seemed if not without limit at least higher than libraries had ever experienced before. The keywords were growth and expansion![1] Competition was for size—more books, more people. To be just, some of this heady growth made up for a much longer period of neglect and it also corresponded with enormous growth in education and research, both of which grew to require resources on an unimaginable scale. Academic libraries struggled to keep up with the proliferation of programs; public libraries with the expanding social goals of federal, state and local governments. The myth of growth as the solution to all problems began to wear thin by the mid 70s and now in the 80s words like cutback and priority have replaced growth and comprehensiveness.[2]

The lack of planning that accompanied the period of expansion is now levying its toll. Because growth was uneven and frequently the result of ad hoc pressures there was no certainty as to what was the core of the library's program. The requirement now is to find the core and restructure library programs to support and promote it as an essential service. This means that libraries must concentrate on what they do best and shuck off services that do not contribute to that goal. Libraries are best qualified to organize and process information, to make it accessible to those who want it. That may appear, on the face of it, to be a license to do all those things libraries have come to encompass during the rich years—teaching—called bibliographic instruction, the development of sophisticated automation systems, staff development on a major scale, planning comprehensive collection development schemes, free on-line searching, multiple branch libraries, specialized services for small groups,—and to some extent all these things are good and necessary but their relationship

---

Murray S. Martin is University Librarian at Tufts University. He is the author of *Budgetary Control in Academic Libraries* and *Issues in Personnel Management in Academic Libraries*, both published by JAI Press.

© 1983 by The Haworth Press, Inc. All rights reserved.

to the central goal has become obscured. Studies have shown that despite proliferating collections libraries frequently do not have available what is required. Other studies[4] have at least brought into question whether it is cost-beneficial to maintain the growth rates that have been built into library mythology. Costs of periodical subscriptions have risen so fast that it is no exaggeration to say they are out of control and threaten to eat up the funds required for other purchases.[5] Automation has not brought the savings that were predicted and it is doubtful whether they will eventuate unless the whole process can take a new direction. All this to serve a contracting community, particularly in higher education, or an impoverished one, in the case of towns and cities.

This may sound exaggerated, but the point must be made and accepted that library growth appears to have over-reached itself and support for it is eroding. When universities have to close whole departments and lay off tenured professors they cannot support expanding libraries. When cities are faced with massive unemployment and shrinking taxes they cannot add to library revenues. Librarians are not the villains but rather victims of their times. Having done what was expected of them in good times with budgets that were seldom adequate they are now expected to achieve much the same results with less. Very few administrators and officials ever bothered to understand the libraries they supported. Libraries can not be turned on and off at will. They depend on continuity in a way that few other institutions do.[6] The simple placing of an order for a book, its cataloging and processing may extend through more than a year. Unlike most industrial products, books are unique items, unamenable to standardized processing. Inventories are not static but grow inexorably over time stretching physical and bibliographical capacities, and this diversity must be organized to be functional. The interrelationship of library functions is not understood nor is their labor-intensive nature. There are multiple reasons why libraries have difficulty in responding to rapid change. Yet with all this libraries have led the way in change.[7] They have more experience with automation than any other part of the University. But change of this magnitude requires great capital expenditure which, by a paradox, is just what is not now available.

Returning to the basic premise, we must ask what libraries must do to survive. First, they must return to their basic role—the collection and organization of information. In fact, libraries could provide the services they are uniquely able to provide if they buy, catalog and circulate materials. This may sound like shock therapy for reference librarians, but the suggestion is not that reference services are unnecessary, only that librarians, as a whole, have overresponded to the growth of information. They are more conscious of the complexity of the information world than any of their users, most of whom care little about how the material got there so long as it is there when they want it.[8] Librarians are among the few professionals who consistently attempt to pass on their skills to those whom they serve. It is unreasonable to suppose that a process that may have taken many years to learn can be passed on to others by simple instruction that has to be crowded in with everything else a student has to cope with. The goal should be the simple teaching of a few basic skills to be accompanied by a new view of library organization which has grown too complex for librarians to comprehend, let alone the user. In addition we should consider whether it would be better to have information ready and packaged rather than direct people to use the tools they barely understand.

Second, libraries must reassess their role within the information world. Despite their imperfections (born of another kind of euphoria) the many commercial services are here to stay. Further, publishing will change substantially over the next 5-6 years in the direction of on-line access and libraries, given their need for careful preparation for change, should now be beginning the process of establishing new relationships, replacing what has frequently been a stormy relationship with cooperation. I do not necessarily believe in the possibility of a paperless society[9] but the roles of paper and electronics will surely change.

Third, libraries must begin to place their money where it is most needed. That is a painful process because it will mean change. Money previously spent for resources may have to be redirected to people and machines. The money for people will almost certainly have to be reallocated between functions. That means some will decline and some will grow. To accomplish changes of this magnitude requires careful financial planning, something libraries have not had much experience with. Ad hoc decisions will not serve.

So much for the rhetoric! What must be done? The first requirement is to attain financial control of the library. That means more than being able to pay for what is being done. It means deciding what must be done and allocating the resources to see that it is done. It means greater accountability on the part of management and it means careful evaluation of what is done.[10] The traditional statistics suitable for growth periods will not serve any more. Decisions on priorities have to be based on knowledge of benefits conferred on the user. Tools such as cost-benefit analysis[11] and zero-base budgeting[12] will become much more widely used, if funds are to be allocated wisely. All this requires a great deal more work on the part of library management and some more personally desirable activities will have to go to make room for it. Librarians are not academics whose goal is essentially personal development but managers responsible for running an expensive enterprise, even though they have the second responsibility of understanding and working with the academic community.[13]

The crucial areas for examination are collection goals, information goals and the ways of restructuring the library to meet them. Growth as a goal in itself cannot be sustained. It is not merely a question of acquiring materials, but of housing and servicing them. Fifty thousand new books a year require a mile of shelving. Are there 50,000 books that could be retired? Almost certainly yes, but deaccessioning (the new word for weeding) costs money. Housing new books, however, costs more money.[14] Furthermore, this kind of contraction requires that users be educated to understand it *and* implies that libraries should be willing to pay for resource sharing.[15]

The budget for materials has to be redefined. It can no longer be seen only as a means for increasing a library's collection. Some of it must go to pay for access elsewhere, whether by contracting for services, providing on-demand copies for personal retention or by supporting interlibrary loan.[16] Yes, it may mean deferred satisfaction on the part of some users, but it can also mean increased satisfaction for a greater proportion if, say, multiple copies are purchased rather than a wide range of less-used materials. It will also mean a surrender of some autonomy, though most libraries already recognize that they cannot be self-sufficient. Cooperative serial and book retention schemes are very complicated to administer, but the computer can be used to make it easier. In fact they have been made more complicated than necessary because the requisite funds were not made available. Even one percent of acquisitions budgets would create a pool of money able to ensure greater access for all. I am aware that this counsel has the same weaknesses as the magic of a Bradford-Zipf distribution. It does not solve the specific decision that will have to be made, but it does point the way towards deciding on the core which each library should maintain.

In the same way, libraries need to re-examine their goals in providing information. Local resources are a large portion of the information available. Their physical and bibliographic organization determines how well they serve their purpose. The average library user is relatively helpless faced with a catalog and resources that are housed in a complex building according to some arcane rule. We cannot expect users to learn the entire classification system, though most of them would be better off if they did. We can now, thanks to the computer, manipulate our bibliographic records so that our obscure symbols become meaningful. We can also look again at the need for multiple shelving sequences and multiple specialized reference centers. While these may have been based on some correct perceptions—for example, no one person can comprehend organization of a collection much larger than 2000 volumes, instead that person automatically breaks a larger collection up into manageable bits and in the process discards many things relevant to his needs—the proliferating pieces are no longer sufficiently connected. The underlying structure has been weakened. In Chinua Achebe's phrase, "Things fall apart." The process of entropy has been carried to extremes in some institutions which now at best represent slightly organized chaos.

The need is to reinforce the center. This may mean the consolidation of all reference services in one place backed up by distant access online, and it may also mean the development of much more sophisticated instructions for using automated catalogs. In this area OCLC has recognized the critical need for upgrading user interface.[17] It certainly means the upgrading of the much neglected circulation function. It certainly requires that information about resources outside the library be made an integral part of the library's own information system. Nina Matheson's landmark study of Health Sciences information needs makes this abundantly clear.[18] My only regret is that it treats these libraries as a closed system. Even in so specialized a field that is no longer possible. The principle, however, of system-to-library, library-to-library and library-to-user networks applies to all libraries.

To achieve such far-reaching goals implies a total reconsideration of library budgets. Expenditures, for example on hardware, software and their maintainance will increase greatly.[19] The increase must be met by new revenue or by decreases in other expenditure. Both are necessary, so we must face up to recovering costs from users for special services while at the same time reassigning people from their present tasks to new ones, the principal one of which is designing and implementing the library-to-user network. Unfortunately we lack standards and guidelines for the process, which presents an admirable opportunity to library schools and professional associations. It is also necessary that foundations and other funding agencies be persuaded of its necessity since the funds required for research are outside the reach of most libraries.

Libraries need, however, to recognize that internal funds must be freed to support internal development. Matheson's disturbing comments on the low priority given to the development of management skills[20] can be extended to all libraries. In addition libraries need to become more aggressive in seeking outside funding for these purposes. The Federal tap has been turned off—temporarily we hope since this is a critical area for the whole economy—and private sources are not yet educated to the need.

Although I remain a strong advocate of central responsibility for budgetary control, it is necessary to expand the role of middle management for program development. Each program in a library should be considered as a project and its manager asked to account for expenditures, subject to central review. The latter is necessary because library programs do not function autonomously. Each unit should, however, present a plan of action which corresponds to its role within the library as a whole.

Such a process can be effective only if the library develops a general statement of purpose, and a set of priorities relating to that statement. This is the role of central management and must be carried out in consultation with the administration, users' representatives, and the staff if it is to carry any weight. The statement of purpose must be supported by mechanisms for determining priorities and making decisions, not only between desirable and undesirable programs, but between equally good programs which cannot be funded from existing budgets. The latter is an unusual course for libraries and for higher education generally, which has tended to meet budget decreases by across-the-board cuts, a measure which most surely signifies poverty of imagination and foredooms the whole library to ineffectiveness. Selective change is the requirement of the day.

Economy in operation is one way of stretching money and several very useful points are available in the publication *Managing Cutbacks* by the Budget, Accounting and Costs Committee of the Library Administration and Management Association. There are limits to these kinds of savings. It is simply not possible continually to reduce staff within a service organization and maintain the desired level of service. Careful examination of automated substitutes for personal labor is another important area, one which requires very careful planning and, usually, the infusion of capital expenditure. But the greatest savings still come from the elimination of unproductive activity and this is where management must turn its closest attention.

The tasks suggested here are heavy ones but not outside the ability of any dedicated manager. There is no single methodology that can apply to every situation, for each has its unique character. If it were not so, then each library would be the replica of another. The differences are what give character and must be preserved in any change, since they have developed in response to the unique characteristics of the institution. Too often it is easier to adopt other people's answers to questions which do not apply in our own case, and such a course must be guarded against. Equally, of course, it is necessary to guard against the perpetuation of useless difference. Here is the field where managers must exercise discrimination in decision-making and be sure of the values by which they make judgments. The guide must be the good of the community served.

NOTES

1. Richard DeGennaro, "Library Statistics and User Satisfaction: No Significant Correlation," *Journal of Academic Librarianship* 6(2):95, May 1980.

2. Daniel Gore has been something of a Cassandra in the library world. Such books as his *Farewell to Alexandria* (Westport, Conn.: Greenwood Press, 1976) have pointed out that there must be some limit to growth, a lesson librarians were slow to heed.

3. Marjorie E. Murfin, "The Myth of Accessibility: Frustration and Failure in Retrieving Periodicals," *Journal of Academic Librarianship.* 6(1): 16-19, March 1980.

4. Allen Kent, and others. *A Cost-Benefit Model of Some Critical Library Operations in Terms of Use of Materials: Final Report.* Pittsburgh: University of Pittsburgh, April 15, 1978. Also the later symposium: The Use of Library Materials: *The University of Pittsburgh Study,* New York: Dekker, 1979, especially chapter 5 by Jacob Cohen.

5. Any cost price-index will reveal this, for example *Price Indexes for 1982: U.S. Periodicals and Serial Services,* by Norman B. Brown and Jone Phillips (Library Journal 107 (14): 1379-1382. Aug. 1982). A more general index is developed in *Higher Education Prices and Price Indexes,* by D. Kent Halstead, formerly published by the G.P.O. and now as a privately published serial.

6. Murray S. Martin, *Budgetary Control in Academic Libraries.* Greenwich, Conn.: JAI Press, 1978, pp. 27, 97-99.

7. Aaron Cohen and Elaine Cohen, "The Quiet Revolution on Campus," *Chronicle of Higher Education* Nov. 25, 1981, p. 56.

8. *Scholarly Communication: The Report of the National Enquiry.* Baltimore: The Johns Hopkins University Press, 1979, pp.5, 92.

9. Frederick Wilfrid Lancaster, *Toward Paperless Information Systems.* New York: Academic Press, 1978.

10. Peter F. Drucker, "Measuring the Public Service Institution," *College and Research Libraries,* 37 (1); p.13, Jan. 1976, and H. William Axford, "Peformance Measures Revisited," *College and Research Libraries,* 34 (5): 244-257, Sept. 1973.

11. Jeffrey A. Raffel and Robert Shishko. *Systematic Analysis of University Libraries: An Application of Cost-Benefit Analysis to the M.I.T. Libraries.* Cambridge: The M.I.T. Press, 1969.

12. Ching-Chin Chen, *Zero-Base Budgeting in Library Management: A Manual for Librarians.* Phoenix, Ariz.: Oryx Press, 1980, and William J. Crowe, "Zero-Base Budgeting for Libraries: A Second Look," *College and Research Libraries,* 43 (1): 47-50, Jan. 1982.

13. This despite the fact that I support academic status for librarians. I feel, however, that it has become an independent goal, little related to the changing conditions in libraries. Fred Duda put it very well when he asked, "Could academic librarians have come to grips with such pressing problems as technological change and library education in the 1970s if less time had been spent on the status of librarians in books, articles, and seemingly endless discourses at ALA Council meetings?" *(College and Research Libraries* 43 (4): 357 (July 1982)).

14. The Lehigh Study of a proposal to sell off the rare book collection (Daniel Traister, "Goodbye to All That: *A Case Study in Deaccessioning."* Wilson Library Bulletin, 56 (a): 663-668) deserves careful study. Do the same rules apply to the rest of the collection? Should policies be changed to prevent the situation from getting worse? These are questions still to be explored. Other articles in the same issue discuss other aspects of deaccessioning.

15. David A. Kronick, "Goodbye to Farewells: Resource Sharing and Cost Sharing," *Journal of Academic Librarianship* 8 (3): 132-136, July 1982.

16. Daniel Gore, "Nothing Succeeds Like Excess: An Essay on Interlibrary Loan," *Library Journal* 107 (14): 1375-1378. Gore makes the valid point that in the long run it costs a great deal more to buy and house a book than to borrow it. He also makes the thought-provoking suggestion that books in low demand might well be transferred to a requesting library which clearly has a use for them.

17. Charles R. Hildreth. *Online Public Access Catalogs: The User Interface.* Dublin, Ohio: OCLC Inc, 1982, Chapter 5.

18. Nina W. Matheson, and others. *Academic Information in the Academic Health Sciences Center: Roles for the Library in Information Management.* Washington, D.C.: Association of American Medical Colleges, April 28, 1982.

19. This is already occurring, as is made clear by the reports of financial expenditures by libraries in the Association of Research Libraries.

20. Matheson, p. 47.

PART I:
GENERAL FINANCIAL PRINCIPLES

Issues in the Financial Management of Research Libraries

Duane E. Webster

I. INTRODUCTION AND BACKGROUND

If academic libraries are to survive as active partners in instruction and research, they must be sensitive to changing conditions both within their internal structure and in the external environment. In the 1980s, a central issue is maintaining quality while dealing with pressing financial problems.

Because research libraries are one part of a larger, interdependent system, we can most effectively study their economic and financial management issues in context of the parent institutions, and the demographic, social, political, and cultural changes that affect higher education and the nation as a whole. The growing severity of financial pressures is motivating research library administrators to take a closer look at relationships within this system, for both practical applications and theoretical knowledge.

The recent high rate of inflation, the need for more equitable library salaries, and the dramatic increase in costs of library materials—combined with relatively stable budget allocations—have moved academic libraries from the period of growth and expansion that characterized the 1960s to a period of stabilization, with the prospect of irreversible deterioration of library capabilities.

Available statistics on research library costs and programs suggest a growing erosion of capability to meet demands because of the effects of inflation, the information explosion, and declining rates of budget growth. For example, the 75 academic libraries that were members of the Association of Research Libraries (ARL) in both 1969-1970 and 1979-1980 reported that during the past decade:

Duane E. Webster is Director of the Office of Management Studies, Association of Research Libraries, Washington, D.C. He has been responsible for developing and operating a national program of management research and assistance to research libraries seeking to improve services, resources and performance. He has written a number of articles on library administration, including a number related to the Management Review and Analysis Program (MRAP). This paper is based upon a presentation entitled "Risk Capital for Library Development" made at the Fourteenth Annual Alumni-in-Residence Program of the University of Michigan, School of Library Science.

© 1983 by The Haworth Press. Inc. All rights reserved.

- Expenditures for library materials increased by 91%, while the gross number of volumes added each year to collections, decreased by 22.5%. During this period the cost of books rose 273% and the cost of periodicals rose 398%.
- The median number of non professional staff grew by 11.5%, with no increase in the number of professional staff. The median expenditures for salaries and wages increased 106%.
- The median number of volumes held increased by 44%, and the annual rate of growth slowed from 7% to 2.9%.
- Operating expenditures doubled during the decade.[1]

As research universities develop long-range financial forecasts covering five years or a decade, library line item costs—if recent trends continue—will grow at a rate faster than increases projected for university income. These cost increases come from a number of sources, including the following: (1) extraordinary increases in the unit cost of published materials, magnified for such libraries because of their need to purchase particularly expensive foreign materials; (2) the well-documented information explosion placing demands upon the library to acquire larger numbers of more expensive materials; (3) a growing demand from faculty and students for more assistance from the professional staff in identifying sources, in sorting out what is relevant, and in locating and acquiring material from many sources; and (4) an emerging communications technology, which provides access to information in a variety of media.

II. CURRENT ECONOMIC CONCERNS

The university budget process is supposedly the means to plan and implement necessary financial changes. But it is no surprise that this budget process, so crucial for so many reasons, is often cumbersome and poorly understood. For example, budgets are difficult to manipulate readily to study the effect of a specific change on the other parts of the budget, and incentives to save money often are lacking. To alleviate some of these problems, universities have introduced various types of systems in recent years—such as zero base budgeting, the Planning-Program Budgeting System (PPBS), and computerized models such as Stanford University's Trade-Offs System (TRADES)—each with its benefits and weaknesses. Everyday decisions must be made using such systems. But, do these systems help people become aware of financial issues? Do they provide incentives for saving money and innovating? Do they truly allocate resources fairly and equitably, permit assessment of the effects of various changes on the university, help insure effective management of resources, and tie resource allocations to goals and objectives? Or, do they merely provide new formats for bureaucratic and political infighting?

When libraries face their part of paring the budget, two paradoxes can arise. Sometimes libraries become victims of their own success: because of enhanced user education and services programs, expectations created within the university may go unmet as financial pressures rise. And in other cases, the very technology and cooperative ventures that could help alleviate tight money problems are not possible because of initially high investment capital requirements. Libraries that do plunge into bibliographic utilities, networks, consortia, and automation often must do so without adequate knowledge of their own needs, cost-benefit relationships of the new development(s), alternative options, and where the development(s) may lead.

The problem of capital renewal deserves attention from three aspects. First is the repair and replacement of library facilities. Institutions have deferred major maintenance, have not renovated buildings, have not replaced or updated equipment, and have not always made needed facilities changes to accommodate the physically disabled. University administrations have sacrificed funding for these ongoing maintenance activities for short term economic gains.

A second part of the problem involves the libraries' collections of published materials. Research library collections have not expanded to contain the same coverage of published literature as in the past. The statistics noted earlier show that universities are not able to meet commitments to information access that are commonly assumed to be part of our mission.

But this inability to do the job we have agreed to do in the area of collections is further compounded by a third aspect—the advancing communication/computer technology. The new technology promises information products and services that research libraries simply cannot afford. The integration of on-line processing, data banks, and decentralized terminals raises serious questions of viability of research libraries if the risk capital is not there to allow expansion.

Clearly the impact of telecommunications and related technolgy will change the relationships of information providers and users. In fact the nature of work at all levels of society in the future will be shaped by computers. A key aspect is the combination of technologies that have been available for a long time. Videodiscs, satellite communication, facsimile transmission, electronic mail and optical character recognition are technologies that libraries are uniquely situated to use and promote. Network information systems already employ some of these tools. And at least one major university, the University of Chicago, has reconfigured the campus electrical system making every outlet a telecommunication link.

The cost of this new technology seems staggering. And viewed in a lump sum amount, it is. But responses to the capital requirements must be imaginative and innovative. One point worth recalling is that universities have moved from a near-zero investment in computers in 1960 to an investment of many million today. Furthermore, the profession has found capital in the past to finance library development from federal support combined with private businesses and foundations such as the Council on Library Resources. There are notable instances of universities investing their own capital in libraries when the purposes were persuasive. Private enterprise has led the way in making available machine-based information services such as Lockheed's Dialog, New York Times Information Bank, and BRS's and SDC's information services. There are many examples of commercially developed automated circulation systems. However, the inescapable conclusion is that federal dollars have provided the major capital in the development of information technology and library innovation. This conclusion collides with the reality of today's political arena—all federal aid to libraries could be wiped out in fiscal year 1983. With this in mind, strategies must look at both external and internal approaches to securing the risk capital for future library development.

III. RESPONSES TO FINANCIAL PRESSURES

To a large extent, the past financial management practices of academic libraries have been characterized by limited fiscal control, unevaluated development of collections, reliance on single source financing, multiple missions, hopeful but not purposeful funding, segmented functions with people working in isolation, and what might be called reactive management. We have been able to succeed without a lot of effort devoted to financial management. In fact, the library is often the best managed unit on campus in spite of our own concerns about underfunding, inadequate staffing levels, and poorly supported collections. In the future, however, renewed efforts must be made to develop and promote more successful financial management. The following are some notions of where efforts and improved thinking are needed:

A. External Strategies

1. The organization of the scholarly information function within the university. We need a broad view of the production, distribution and use of information within the university. We can no longer afford to see the library, the computer center, the instructional materials center, the university press, and the bookstore as separate functions to be administered in isolation. Universities will be making important capital decisions that require understanding of the technology and information needs of the future. An example is the development of numeric data bases. Here vast stores of data may be available to support research, yet costs of collecting and disseminating this information are beyond library means and, in most cases, no one takes the responsibility for organizing and providing access. And the costs of expertise and equipment required to manage this material can be enormous. The total information resources of a university need to be organized and managed on a scale comparable to the other major intellectual, physical and fiscal resources. Furthermore, librarians have perspective and understanding that can contribute to quality decisions in this area.

2. *Support from private foundations and industry.* Increasingly, research libraries are turning to external sources for financial help. In the past, foundations and industry often assisted with new buildings or special collections. Increasingly however, library directors devote a major percentage of their time to helping university development officers and private donors understand the investment opportunities libraries present. These opportunities include: funding of critical and visible positions such as specialized bibliographers or key executives; maintenance, renewal, or creation of important portions of basic collections; provision of new automated services and capabilities; and renovation of facilities. The library director as a promoter is often replacing the traditional role of bookman.

An important hope for the future continues to be the Council on Library Resources. This agency has been the single more important facility for library risk capital and has supported some of the more innovative and successful development efforts such as Project Intrex, the College Library/Bibliographic Instruction Experiment and the Barrows Preservation Laboratory. The future holds additional promise for innovative efforts by the Council in bibliographic control, recruitment and development of professional staff, library services and management, and relations with the academic community.

Many higher education administrators view large corporate foundations as important sources for future risk capital. However, although these agencies are receiving more attention because of reduced federal funding, obtaining support from them remains difficult. The OMS, for example, is trying to secure support for a public service study from a major corporate foundation. But the lack of past experience and interest in libraries is proving to be a major obstacle to winning this support. Regional and local foundations which have supported local institutions in the past seem a more inviting target for most libraries.

A recent article in *Science* described the development of collaborative links between universities and industry.[2] Some of these links have encompassed technical education as well as the development of new technology. On one level industry relies on universities for preparation of technicians, and has benefited from university-based research and development. In the area of computer electronics for example, there has been considerable collaboration, and similar arrangements have been developed in the area of genetics. The possibility of new links with industry may provide opportunities for libraries to play an important role and to gain additional financial support.

Access to large amounts of capital may best be arranged through organizations that group and deploy library resources effectively on a broad scale. For example, members of ARL last year spent over $218 million on library materials. Perhaps a portion of this allocation could be diverted to risk capital to support development of new library systems. This is being done in one way by the members of the Research Libraries Group. To survive, libraries must sacrifice automony; and more might be done on regional or national bases in the areas of bibliographic control, preservation, storage of lesser-used items, and establishing and maintaining telecommunication links.

3. *Understanding the nature and magnitude of universities' financial, intellectual, and capital investment in their libraries.* Management decisions affecting libraries often must be made with incomplete or inadequate information about the immediate and long-term effects on the library, its users, the university, and the nation. Decision making is hampered by lack of information on such topics; the real costs of cooperative enterprises, the values of different forms and types of information, what information users need and use, what factors really drive library costs, what opportunities exist to alter library procedures, costs of those options, and where they might lead.

Some library and university administrators are quite concerned because they have no real information about the effects of library cutbacks of the past ten years. Faculty in the sciences, because they depend heavily on current information, complain about lack of adequate resources. Faculty in other disciplines rely more on older materials and may be relatively content with the collections that have been built up over the years. But some time in the future these faculty, too, will recognize the erosion of collections which has occurred because of cutbacks and loss of purchasing power.

The profession needs visionary policy makers who can see beyond immediate institutional requirements while understanding institutional roles. Both public and private funding sources must recognize the need to finance fundamental change in academic libraries, for without new money for capital development, libraries face a grim future.

B. Internal Strategies

On an internal basis a series of tradeoffs must be made. The library can't continue to be all things to all people. Contribution and performance can't be assumed; they must be managed. The following ideas can be used to tighten internal financial and organizational management.

1. Demonstrating relationships among library costs and contributions to university programs and decisions. The library can no longer be an assumed good. Like other ingredients in a recipe for excellence, the library must demonstrate the quality of staff and collections, a good sense of the market, and a clear understanding of program priorities which are well communicated. Library managers must establish which current university financial pressures, program trends, and decisions most affect library costs. They need to study the impact of university program decisions on library planning and operations. They need to identify the major tradeoffs in terms of library operations and to present their case with information that will strengthen the university-wide decision process.

2. Rethinking internal library organization and staffing patterns. The research library plays roles at both the institutional and national levels. Some financial problems arise from trying to serve both roles; other problems arise because those roles are constantly undergoing change. For example, research libraries, while accepting limitations in their ability to develop collections, have done little to rationalize or distribute responsibility for operating collections on a regional or national basis. In another area, most libraries still view their objective as maintaining optimal bibliographic access to their collections to the point of not accepting cataloging data from peer institutions. This leads to expensive bibliographic systems that may meet local requirements or traditions but are increasingly uneconomical.

Libraries face the prospect of severe degradation of performance if they simply try to refine and tighten while maintaining the full array of traditional objectives. The pressures faced by research libraries call for rethinking these objectives and marshalling resources to do fewer things well.

The job of organizational development starts with asking what people are doing, whether it is necessary, and what would happen if it were not being done.

After we have rethought our objectives and functions we need to examine the distribution of functions and how they are integrated. Functional specialization is a traditional organizational format which can create a number of staffing and organizational problems such as provincialism, rivalry, limited awareness of contribution and interrelatedness, resistance to change, short-term perspectives, and poor communication. In a period of rapid change, more flexible and responsive structures such as product-oriented, team-centered, and matrix organizations can work better than functional forms of organization.

3. Innovative funding and budgeting. Most successful organizations manage their budgets to encourage innovation and development as critical components. Libraries rarely do this. In fact, analytical processes involved in budget planning and implementation often are not what they should be, and the relationship of library expenditures to academic and research program expenditures is often ignored or poorly understood. Library allocations based on either history or a formula based on enrollment are usually inadequate.

Experimenting with more effective ways to cope with current economic pressures is one response. How can budget monitoring be employed to control costs? Can long-range planning effectively take account of cost saving methods and economies of scale? How can the costs of interdependence, cooperation and shifts to automated systems be assessed? Should libraries develop new sources of support? Rice University, for example, provides business information services including computer literature services, document delivery, telefacsimile transmission, corporate borrowing servivces, SDI, and reference services that recover costs at the rate of $25,000 annually.

The issue of charging fees for services is a product of technological expansion and declining support levels. The use of fees defrays the costs of providing a wide range of innovative services, they reflect and ration demand for these services, and they provide a measure of the relative value of various library services. The responses needed in this area are development of alternative sources of financing and exploration of the purposeful funding of activities.

4. *Internal development of risk capital for innovation.* Many of the possible solutions to the economic problems of research libraries involve large amounts of capital—capital for applications of technology, transition to new systems, development of new management tools, initiation and enhancement of cooperative ventures. These investments appear beyond the reach of the individual institution.

In fact, most libraries do not consciously allocate monies for research and development yet there are options for locating internal funds for risk capital including shifting collection funds and staff funds. For the most part libraries do not have a great deal of flexibility for reallocating funds, although private institutions are somewhat more progressive in this respect than public. While 10 to 15% is the maximum size of most discretionary funds, even with these small amounts libraries can make some efforts. For example, word processing is inexpensive but can have significant impact on office productivity and intellectual efforts.

5. *Internal control and monitoring.* The use of analytical information for decision making must be expanded. Over the last few years, university administrators and library directors have sought more and improved analytical information for making important management decisions related to library operations and development.

Financial reporting systems rooted in the past often do not reveal problems until the organization is in trouble and do not report information the way managers use information. One answer is to develop a few crucial and sensitive financial measures in combination with non-financial measures of output such as productivity measures. In developing a better understanding of research library costs, a number of questions need to be answered such as: What are the major costs, and how do they change? What external factors most affect library costs? What sources of information are available on costs? How is the information used for decision-making? What major tradeoffs affect budget construction? What steps can be taken to improve cost information for decision-making? What options and ideas exist for controlling current and long-run costs?

IV. CONCLUSION

A paradox faces academic and research libraries. The financial requirements for libraries to simply survive and uphold present responsibilities are staggering. Yet it is clear that libraries must convert to a new age of information access and use if they are to be a viable part of the scholarly process. The answer to this dilemma appears to be in part new strategies of financial management and organizational development.

We need to understand the capital requirements for the next decade and communicate those needs to the decision makers in universities, government, foundations and the corporate sector. The way universities organize the production and use of scholarly information should be recast. Private sources and cooperative agencies should be the centers for innovative development. And internal library management should be tougher and more demanding while encouraging staff involvement and growth.

Organizations can grow even in periods of financial constraints. What is needed is optimism in developing a vital new library concept and the aggressive pursuit of an influential role in institutional decision-making.

Journal issues such as this one and joint meetings of library and university administrators and economists such as one sponsored in October 1981 by the Association of Research Libraries (ARL) and the Research Libraries Group, Inc. can help focus attention on economic issues of research libraries within the framework of higher education finance, and can help create a common basis of understanding among people who have the knowledge and power to help solve the problems. The two papers that follow were presented at the meeting mentioned above, where 18 university academic and administrative officers, library directors, economists, and management specialists met in Washington, D.C. on October 14, 1981 to explore issues related to the economics and financial management of research libraries. The meeting, supported by the Council on Library Resources, was unique in terms of the several points of view represented, but the issues considered are probably quite familiar to those committed to research library improvement. A report of these discussions is available.[3]

REFERENCES

1. Association of Research Libraries. *ARL Statistics, 1979-80.* Washington, D.C., Author; 1980, p. 2.
2. J. G. Linvill, "University Role in the Computer Age." *Science* vol. 215 #4534, February 12, 1981, p. 802-807.
3. Duane Webster and Keith Russell *The Economics and Financial Management of Research Libraries: A Report on an Exploratory Meeting.* Washington, D.C.: Association of Research Libraries/OMS, 1982.

Financial Planning Needs of Publicly-Supported Academic Libraries in the 1980s: Politics as Usual

Edward R. Johnson

INTRODUCTION

In the Spring of 1982 I was asked to write an article on the subject of financial planning for the 1980s from the perspective of the publicly-supported medium-sized academic library. As I reviewed the topic I began to realize that being in Texas, where higher education currently is not quite in the same dire straits as the rest of the nation, perhaps my view was too narrow. Further, as I read the literature of academic librarianship and higher education, it seemed to me that the picture in regard to academic library finances today is confusing and sometimes contradictory because of the wide variance of perceptions from campus to campus.

Therefore, in order to gather information and put my own ideas into proper perspective, I took the tried-and-true approach of sending out a questionnaire. In mailing this questionnaire I was well aware of the limitations of survey research but I also believed that this approach had several potential benefits as well. It was not my intention to compile a large amount of data to test for statistical significance. Instead, I was attempting to find out what my fellow library administrators' views are on a number of questions of concern to me. Their answers are illuminating, sometimes surprising. They occasionally agree with my own opinions, sometimes not.

THE INSTITUTIONS SURVEYED

Quite often in recent years we have read numerous opinion and attitude surveys of member librarians of the Association of Research Libraries (ARL). There were several such surveys, for example, reported at the second ACRL Conference in Minneapolis in 1981. What is surprising is the

---

Edward R. Johnson is currently the Director of Libraries, North Texas State University Library, and holds a PhD degree in Library Science from the University of Wisconsin. He recently co-authored *Organizational Development for Academic Libraries: an Evaluation of the Management Review and Analysis Program* (Greenwood Press, 1980).

© 1983 by The Haworth Press, Inc. All rights reserved.

paucity of similar survey research among members of the larger Association for College and Research Libraries (ACRL). Surely the opinions and attitudes of this substantial group of librarians is as important, if perhaps not as influential, as that of the ARL.

Accordingly, fifty-five libraries of publicly-supported institutions of higher education were identified as participants in the survey. These institutions are characterized by the Carnegie Council as "doctorate-granting universities I and II" (as is North Texas State University).[1] Most of the members of the Association for Research Libraries, on the other hand,. are characterized by the Carnegie Council as "comprehensive research universities."

Thirty-eight of the fifty-five questionnaires were returned for a response rate of 69.1 percent. Of the thirty-eight institutions represented by the questionnaires, seven libraries are members of the Association of Research Libraries while 31 were members only of ACRL. The enrollments of the thirty-eight universities (in 1976) ranged from 6,103 students to 38,400 students for an average enrollment of 15,798 students. This figure is comparable to the enrollment of North Texas State University for the same period—17,018 students. Thus, the libraries selected for the survey seem quite similar in size, composition, and mission to that of my own institution.

THE QUESTIONNAIRE

The academic library administrators were asked thirteen closed-ended questions and were told to respond using a five-point scale ("greatly decrease" to "greatly increase," "1" to "5" etc.). In addition, they were also asked two open-ended questions. The responses to the closed-ended questions are reported according to frequency of response. (Not all questions were answered by all respondents so none of the total equals thirty-eight.) For further analysis, some of the questions were assigned a weight of one to five. These weights were then multiplied times the number of responses to generate a ranked list. The results of the open-ended questions are analyzed last.

THE RESPONSES—CLOSE-ENDED QUESTIONS

When asked "what do you predict are the funding prospects for your library during the next ten years?" twenty respondents replied "modest increase." Ten predicted "relative stability" and five "a slight decrease." Only one librarian foresaw a "great increase" and another predicted a "great decrease." The librarians were then asked if this predicted pattern would "be sufficient to meet the needs of the library in its mission of supporting the university's teaching and research needs." Twenty-six replied "less than sufficient" while one saw it as "more than sufficient," ten as sufficient," and only two as "greatly insufficient."

The next question asked, "in your opinion, what will happen to the library's share of the university's education and general budget in the next ten years?" The respondents were almost evenly divided between "relative stability" (fifteen) and "modestly increase" (thirteen). Seven people, however, predicted "slightly decrease" while only two foresaw "greatly increase."

The librarians were then asked to rate eleven areas of the library's budget "in terms of their importance over the next ten years." A few of the respondents expressed confusion over the meaning of the word "importance" in this context. The question was intended to elicit the areas of concern that will receive the most attention from library administrators. The responses are listed in order, with the first being of "greatest importance" and the last of "least importance." The number in parentheses indicates the weighted ranking:

"Most Important" Areas of the Library's Budget

1. Cost of periodicals (171)
2. Cost of books (166)
3. Cost of equipment (152)
4. Librarian salaries (137)
5. Staff salaries (132)
6. Cost of audio/visual materials (113)
7. Cost of supplies (111)
8. Cost of binding (94)
9. Part-time salaries (85)
10. Cost of maintenance and repair (84)
11. Cost of custodial services (69)
12. Other—cost and need for professional development; telecommunication costs; costs related to comprehensive information access; and matching dollars for external funding (one response each.)

The librarians were then asked "what areas of the university budget are of most concern to your institution's top administrators?" The responses are listed in order of importance from "greatest" to "least." The number in parentheses indicates the weighted rankings:

"Most Important" Areas of the University's Budget

1. Organized research (141)
2. Automation (130)
3. Faculty salaries (118)
4. Periodical subscriptions (76)

5. Books to be purchased (74)
6. Equipment, including automation (71)
7. Binding (67)
8. Staff positions (65)
9. Librarian positions (61)
10. Supplies (57)
11. Maintenance and repair (48)

Almost all librarians (thirty-two) replied "yes" when asked "do you plan to attempt tapping alternative sources of funds in the future (e.g., other than from regular source of appropriations)?" Only one person replied negatively and three were unsure. The thirty-two librarians planning to tap alternative sources of funds listed those sources in the order listed below. Number one is of the "most likely benefit to the library budget." The number in parentheses indicates the weighted rankings:

Alternative Sources of Funds to be Tapped

1. Private donations (122)
2. Supplemental funds from university administration (117)
3. Foundations (106)
4. "Friends of the Library" organizations (102)
5. Other—grants (two responses); government grants (one response.)

Looking ahead, the librarians were asked to assess "what future developments in the university are likely to have the greatest impact on the budget process that will also affect the library." The respondents were asked to rank seven items "in order of importance." Again, this word caused some confusion but the resulting rankings seem to indicate the respondents' sense of priorities. The items below are listed in order of "importance of impact" on the library budget, with number one being most important. The number listed in parentheses indicates the weighted rankings:

Future Developments to Have Greatest Impact on the Budget Process

1. Enrollment (150)
2. Automation (127)
3. Curriculum (111)
4. Inter-Institutional Cooperation (104)
5. Governance (92)
6. Alumni Relations (90)
7. Athletics (60)
8. Other—demands of non-library constituencies; state income (one response each.)

Twenty-six librarians stated that their institution "is presently engaged in a formal planning process" or plans "to initiate one soon." Only one person replied negatively to this question and one person was unsure. Ten, however, did not answer the question. When asked "is the library presently engaged in a formal planning process or does it plan to initiate one soon?" thirty-one respondents replied in the affirmative. Only four answered "no" and two were unsure. Finally, twenty respondents believed that formal planning is going to be "very important for library administrators in the next ten years." Twelve librarians believed that it will be "important" and only one thought that it will be "unimportant." Three respondents were unsure about their answer.

THE RESPONSES—OPEN-ENDED QUESTIONS

The respondents were asked to list their three "major concerns in regard to the library budget and financial planning for the next ten years." Their answers were combined into eleven categories. These categories reflect the common theme of the respondents' concerns. They are also used because most of the respondents did not use complete sentences and few elaborated on their brief answers. The concerns of the librarians are listed in order of frequency of response. The number in parentheses indicates the number of responses:

Major Concerns About the Library Budget and Financial Planning

1. Maintaining or improving collection development despite inflationary costs of library materials, especially periodicals and serials (22).
2. Automation and utilization of technological advances (21):
   —funding
   —problems
   —impact on personnel, services, organization
   —goals and objectives.
3. Economic problems in addition to the inflationary costs of library materials (19):
   —economic health of state and nation
   —inflation
   —reduction of federal support
   —effect of cutbacks on staff and budget
   —competition for available funds and supplemental funds
   —declining enrollments
   —need for more private donations.
4. Improving physical facilities and equipment (10):
   —space problems
   —need for new equipment

—lack of funds to replace equipment.
5. Maintaining or improving librarians' salaries (7).
6. Planning (6):
   —expertise needed
   —reallocating resources
   —setting library goals
   —setting university goals.
7. Interlibrary cooperation and resource sharing (6):
   —impact on individual libraries
   —priorities
   —finding methods to improve
   —developing realistic plans.
8. Status and role of librarians (3).
9. "Political" problems (3):
   —"deadwood" faculty and staff
   —credibility of library with administration
   —legislative impact on the institution.
10. Preservation of library materials (1).

Finally, the last question was "what advice or recommendations do you have for your academic librarian colleagues that might help them to cope with the problems of the 1980s?" The answers ranged from a terse "a clear crystal ball" to a cheerful farewell: "Good luck! I'm retiring in June." The several other responses are grouped below by rough category and more or less according to frequency of response:

1. Politics:

   — faculty support: get the backing of the faculty library committee in austerity moves; they can be of great help; the librarians always have friends among the faculty; form useful alliances . . . to increase library's clout; assure their understanding of the financial problems . . . and their support;
   — administrative relationships: get information to the University administration as early and as often as necessary; work closely . . . to hold their confidence in the library's importance and its effectiveness . . . . ; "the library's needs must be kept constantly within the consciousness of the University administration;"
   — public relations: become better salespersons and lobbyists; advertise, get items in the school newspaper, the University bulletin, etc.; promote your successes; "you must be a political creature to survive the 80's."

2. Management and Planning

— be a good manager, eliminate unsound practices;
— dynamic leadership, positive attitude, team work, improved management skills and greater awareness of challenges as well as opportunities will be required to do a better job in the 1980's;
— try to get your budget as flexible as possible for the possibility of transfers from one line to the other;
— finalize planning functions and recruit staff competent to plan and evaluate library programs;
— become much more entrepreneurial. Know budgets, budget planning. Libraries must be run as businesses—as complex organizations;
— libraries must continue to manage intelligent change through wise choices. Areas which will need wise choices include: type of people hired, choice of services to achieve our library goals, wise choices in collection building.

3. Cooperation and Resource Sharing:

— work together to establish national priorities;
— enter meaningful resource sharing and document delivery activities;
— investigate every possibility for resource-sharing—materials, technology, staff, whatever;
— establish national guidelines for inter-institutional resource-sharing;
— "for more years than most of us have been working in libraries, librarians have been talking about interlibrary cooperation."

4. Attitude Adjustment:

— try to forget the quantitative goals of the past;
— sharpen . . . pencils and learn how to do more with less;
— be realistic and practical;
— unless conditions are hopeless, forget about building. Utilize what you have to best advantage;
— be very ready to accept change;
— work . . . to get library's "fair share" but recognize that there are also other areas to be served.

5. Alternatives:

— hold your nose and plunge ahead. Creativity is required and it will lead to some failures, but the risks must be taken;
— look for alternatives in funding and space utilization;
— clarify role of private funding agencies such as Council on Library Resources;

— go for private funds with the help of your development office;
— explore external sources of funding.

6. Library Staff:

— increase staff quality and effectiveness;
— work closely with the . . . staff to assure their understanding of budgetary limitations, their suggestions about where adjustments or reallocations can be made, their continued dedication and effort to provide high quality service;
— keep in mind the importance of preserving the availability of librarian expertise and the support of qualified staff;
— build permanent staff now so there is something to fall back on when temporary wages are cut back with increases in minimum wages, reduction of work/study assistance, etc.

7. Other:

— be careful about adopting expensive automation procedures;
— argue that expenditures on automation will ultimately result in more efficiency with less staff (although that is not necessarily so);
— keep the book budget in balance, serials to books;
— convert binding to microfilm/fiche for economy and storage potential;
— accept microformatting as inevitable;
— weed ruthlessly.

SUMMARY OF RESPONSES

The answers of the thirty-eight library administrators responding to the questionnaire show considerable variation in views toward the current economic climate for academic libraries. Most expect to see their budgets continue to increase modestly but some see greater increases while a few others predict no change or some slight decrease in library finances. These responses seem to agree with Harvard's David A. Garvin who predicted that the next decade will be a period in which "the rich get richer while the others scramble to remain solvent . . . . "[2] Most of the respondents expect only modest increases in their budgets or relative stability in the next ten years. Two-thirds of the librarians surveyed do not believe that the funding prospects will be sufficient to meet the university's needs.

Adding to this cautious view of the financial future is the fact that most of the academic library administrators surveyed believe their institution is putting more emphasis on organized research, automation, and faculty salaries than on the library. (But not, thankfully, on intercollegiate athletics.) These librarians are planning to search for alternative sources of funds, with private donations and supplemental funds from the university administration viewed as most potentially beneficial. Foundations and friends of the library groups are seen as somewhat less important.

The library administrators in this survey expect enrollment to be the most important future development to have an impact on the budget process. When asked about such future developments, the respondents were also asked whether these developments would have a negative, neutral, or positive influence on the budget. Most skipped this question (probably because it was not well worded) and the results are therefore not very useful. It does seem clear, however, that enrollment is viewed as a positive or a negative influence depending upon whether it increases or decreases. It is also apparent from the answers that institutions are experiencing many different patterns in regard to enrollment.

Automation is also viewed as a significant future development on budget planning. Among those who answered this question, automation is considered to be a highly positive influence. It is not clear from the responses how many institutions are engaged in university-wide formal planning, although it appears that most are. On the other hand, almost all of the library administrators surveyed are engaged in a planning process or will initiate one soon. The overwhelming majority believe that such planning is important.

In regard to their major concerns about budgeting and planning for the next decade, as one would expect, the librarians are most worried about maintaining their library collections. Inflation is viewed as a problem and it continues to be the major problem in buying periodicals. The introduction of automation is considered to be almost as important a concern as collection development, however.

When asked for their advice, the academic library administrators surveyed had few surprises to offer by way of suggestions to their colleagues. We are urged to be good managers while being good campus politicians. They recommend that support from the university administration continues to require careful attention and the faculty are still our best ally. Risk-taking is required more in the future, according to some, and they suggest that we must try to be more creative. The librarians and support staff need to be involved in budgeting and planning as well, in the view of some of the respondents.

It appears to several administrators that we need to accept our financial situation, to learn how to cope with it, to reduce our expectations somewhat, and to be more realistic about the library's place in the environment of competition for resources. Finally, while still elusive, cooperation and resource sharing remain highly desirable goals. One librarian, for example, hopes that:

Joint approval plan profiles, mutual holdings of journal subscriptions, coordinated reference services, etc. will be good for the libraries in terms of a greater economic effectiveness in stretching existing dollars, but such activities will also have the benefit of leading the way into more extensive and non-library cooperation. It can bring academic departments together, first for library cooperation, and then later perhaps for other things.

CONCLUSIONS

The data I received from my fellow administrators of medium-sized academic libraries confirmed my initial impression. The financial picture for publicly-supported academic institutions in the United States today is confusing because there is great variance from region to region. Some of my colleagues are indeed having the bleak problems due to lack of funding that have been mentioned in the press. A few others, on the other hand, are doing surprisingly well and are generally optimistic about the future. The majority are apparently in a situation somewhere in between these two extremes.

In Texas, for example, the state Coordinating Board for Higher Education has recommended a substantial increase in the library formula. This increase, coupled with enrollment gains (upon which the formula is based), means that many academic librarians in Texas are hoping for significant budget increases for 1983/84–1984/85. Most administrators of publicly-supported medium-sized academic libraries in the United States, however, expect only moderate increases during the next decade. In any event, the majority of librarians whom I surveyed believe that the funds available to them will not be sufficient to meet the teaching and research needs of their institutions in the 1980s.

This is a disturbing finding although not a surprising one. We have been told for some time by scholars and reporters alike about academia's financial problems. W. John Minter and Howard Bowen have described the seventies and eighties in higher education as a period of "sustained financial stringency." Minter and Bowen, while finding that public institutions are suffering from reductions in state funding, have also concluded, however, that there "is little evidence of retrenchment" in academic programs.[3] Financial disaster has been staved off by deferring building maintenance, cutting energy consumption, reducing the real compensation of faculty and staff, maintaining enrollment, and holding down library budgets.

"Genteel poverty" is a phrase used in recent years to describe the financial prospects for most academic libraries. While this is a loathsome phrase to many of us, it seems that a number of academic library administrators are accepting this situation as more or less inevitable. But, it is hopeful to note, library administrators are also seeking innovative ways to increase non-traditional financial support for the library, looking for other alternative solutions, involving their librarians and staff in decision-making, and trying to improve the daily management of their libraries.

Librarians believe that more effective management and planning will result in better efficiency in using the library's resources. Most, however, seem also to be reconciled to economic realities in which libraries have to compete for funds with other units on campus. Library administrators are apparently reexamining their attitudes and recognizing that the "library's share" has to be considered in light of the economic problems besetting all of the university. In other words, with a few exceptions the expectations of academic librarians seem to be lowering somewhat. Unfortunately, such attitude adjustment may also reflect the regret and perhaps the "despair" of librarians over the "benign neglect" which William A. Moffett has recently found still pervading academia about the library. He concludes that "apathy and misunderstanding are still prevalent problems today . . . " among university administrators.[4]

RECOMMENDATIONS

1. Fund Raising. A personal surprise from the survey was that supplemental funds from the university are considered to be almost as important sources as private donations. Given the intense competition among campus units, the widespread problem of inflation, and the scramble for money for more automation, my own observation is that the library is not in a particularly advantageous position competitively. Perhaps my institution is unusual, facing as it does another deficit year due to not enough money for maintenance and operation and too much money spent on football. Unfortunately, I am afraid that it is not.

Further, the trend today in institutional development is "distributed fund-raising." The Development Office no longer believes that it is the sole agency on campus that is responsible for finding money from alternative sources. Academic deans—and librarians—in the 1980s are going to be required increasingly to raise additional funds on their own. For librarians this need not be highly traumatic as there are many friends and alumni of universities who are willing to buy books but not athletes. The development professionals are invaluable and their expertise should be enlisted in the library's cause.

2. Planning. It was heartening to find that nearly all the library administrators surveyed are engaged in some sort of planning effort although it was not asked exactly what this "effort" entails. Planning is increasingly being recognized as an important tool for coping with financial stringency. The growing use by academic librarians of defining goals and objectives, writing mission statements and five-year plans, and utilizing consultants are important strategies for the next decade. The Office of Management Studies of the Association of Research Libraries has found, however, that "less attention is paid to the fit of the library within the university budget, and the analytical processes involved in budget planning and implementation. Competing interests within the university are important in this consideration, as well as the relationship of library expenditures to academic and research program expenditures."[5]

William Moffet believes that communication and consultation on campus are being hampered by the organization of the central administration. "The librarian," he writes, "is also less likely to participate in institutional decision-making."[6] The challenge, then, for academic library administrators is to merge their planning efforts with those of the university. It may seem obvious, but it bears repeating, that the most important goal for the library administrator is to insure a role for himself or herself in university-wide planning and decision-making. Admittedly, this is an easy recommendation to make but one which will be extremely challenging to achieve.

3. Automation. It is surprising how widespread automation has become on the typical university campus. Computers of all sizes are everywhere, from the print shop and the bookstore to food services and the physical plant. Automated information systems provide information for scheduling, budgeting, research proposals, enrollment, textbook purchasing, temperature control, and so on. "At the same time the administration of the academic institution is also collecting and processing a wealth of information which is relevant to the planning and management of the academic library."[7] Management information is thus just as important a goal for automation in the academic library as are reference, acquisitions, cataloging, serials, and other programs.

It was evident from the survey that automation expenses are seen as only slightly less important in university budgeting than organized research. Academic library administrators predict that only enrollment will have a greater impact than automation on the university's budget in the next ten years. Furthermore, they see this development as having a highly positive influence. Many institutional administrators are intrigued by the apparent "affinity" between the library and the computer center. So, librarians need to be in the forefront of automation development on campus or, surely, they will find someone else doing it for them.[8]

4. Resource sharing. One minor surprise from the survey was the strong support given for interlibrary cooperation and resource sharing. Academic library administrators are concerned about the costs of such activities and the potential strain on their budgets. On the other hand, they urge further regional and national efforts to determine priorities and to develop realistic plans. Throughout the comments of these librarians runs a theme of utilizing technology and working harder to move resource-sharing from the talked-about stage to the implementation stage. "While there are any number of real instances of genuine cooperation," writes one library administrator, "some of the talk has been just that—and no more. The economies we all face in the future will require that we rethink our cooperative efforts, improve on them, and undertake even more by way of cooperation than we have in the past."

Interinstitutional cooperation, as we all know, has many unresolved problems and many critics. It is certainly not a panacea. But the administrators of a number of medium-sized academic libraries believe that access to other, perhaps collectively held, information resources holds considerable promise for alleviating academic library poverty in the 1980s. University presidents need to be persuaded that scholarship can be greatly assisted by such cooperative efforts. Their librarians need to convince them that inter-institutional cooperation requires more than moral support.

5. *Politics.* Much of the advice provided to their colleagues by the librarians included in this survey is political in nature. To be a good campus politician is good advice indeed. As Minter and Bowen point out regarding academic programs, "what happens . . . becomes a political decision rather than a financial happening."[9] Perhaps more than anyone else on campus, library administrators are acutely aware of the need to accomplish their goals through good personal relationships. Librarians in general, seeing the university from their broad perspective, are aware of the competition and the tensions between departments and among faculty and administrators. Librarians, of course, are also aware of the crucially central role of the library. As Ralph Ellsworth said twenty years ago: "The moment libraries cease to be problems to university presidents the time will have arrived when scholarship is dead."[10]

Unfortunately, those who control the purse strings do not always recognize the library's importance. Moffett's recent article reports eloquently on the problem:

> Librarians do not invariably find the characteristics they wish their teaching and research colleagues to have: 1) a genuine understanding of the library's mission in higher education, 2) a clearer recognition of the professional librarian's craft and an acceptance of the librarian as a peer in the educational enterprise, and 3) a reliable flow of communication and consultation.[11]

It is up to librarians to impart these values to their colleagues in university administration. As one library administrator in the survey observed, "this can be done effectively in a number of ways and using a number of committees and people. It is a subtle rather than a confrontational thing. Good personal relationships with Deans and Vice Presidents mean a lot.

Stress has to be placed more on the important and positive things rather than on what cannot be done because of the lack of money."

By being deeply involved in academic life—teaching, research, service, as well as librarianship—librarians demonstrate the centrality of their function to the university's mission. As good stewards of the resources under their direction and as implementors of innovative methods and technology, librarians demonstrate to the faculty (who are weak friends but powerful enemies) and administration that the library is a vital place of information not just a dusty warehouse of books. The economically depressed 1980s, when so many institutions of higher education are forced to reassess their priorities, is a crucial time for librarians to do better what they have always tried to do well: to impress upon university administrators the goals and objectives of good academic librarianship; in other words, to be good campus politicians.

NOTES

1. Carnegie Council on Policy Studies in Higher Education. A *Classification of Institutions of Higher Education*. rev. ed. (Berkeley: Carnegie Foundation for the Advancement of Teaching, 1976.)

2. Malcolm G. Scully, "Prediction for the 80's: Rich Colleges Will Get Richer," *Chronicle of Higher Education*, 23(January 13, 1982), p. 14.

3. W. John Minter and Howard R. Bowen, "The Minter-Bowen Report, Part I," *Chronicle of Higher Education*, 24(May 12, 1982), pp. 5-6.

4. William A. Moffett, "Don't Shelve Your College Librarian," *Educational Record*, 63(Summer, 1982), p. 46.

5. "A Precis for the Exploratory Meeting on the Economics and Financial Management of Research Libraries," unpublished paper, Association of Research Libraries, Office of Management Studies, October 14, 1981.

6. Moffett, "Don't Shelve Your College Librarian," p. 49.

7. Michael Bommer and Ronald Chorba, "Academic Library Decision Support Systems," unpublished paper, 1981, p. 2.

8. Moffett, "Don't Shelve Your College Librarian," p. 49.

9. Minter and Bowen, "The Minter-Bowen Report," p. 7.

10. Ralph E. Ellsworth, "The Changing Role of the University Library," *Cornell University Library Conference and Dedication*, (October, 1962), p. 81.

11. Moffett, "Don't Shelve Your College Librarian," p. 49.

Planning and Finance: A Strategic Level Model of the University Library

Jerome Yavarkovsky

INTRODUCTION

Three levels of management information can be considered necessary for effective governance of the university research library, corresponding to three identifiable but not absolutely discrete levels of decision making—strategic planning, management control, and operational control.[1]

Strategic level decisions address general resource allocations and policy. Budgetary reductions, inflationary forces, technological processing opportunities, major gift possibilities, new academic programs—conditions which will affect general program staffing or collecting policies—are given consideration at the strategic level. The overall health and goals of the library as determined by the availability of funds necessary to attain them, are strategic planning concerns.

Management control level decisions are concerned with program resource allocations and policy. The introduction of new services requiring additional staff is an example. The staff may be added to the library roster or shifted from one part of the roster to another, in the latter case with some impact on the department giving up the staff. The relative value of the new service and the lost old service, represented as savings or as opportunity cost, are taken into account at the management control level. It is here that strategic decisions are given form as implementation choices. Other examples are changes in book fund allocations resulting from inflationary forces or increased university appropriations; the introduction of card catalog alternatives as a result of computer based cataloging; adoption of vendor service plans for acquisitions processing so as to reduce acquisitions costs.

Jerome Yavarkovsky is Assistant University Librarian for Planning, Columbia University, New York, NY 10027. This paper was prepared as background for "The Economics and Financial Management of Research Libraries: An Exploratory Meeting," sponsored by The Association of Research Libraries and The Research Libraries Group, Inc., with the support of the Council on Library Resources, Inc., Washington, D.C., October 14, 1981. Heike Kordish and Thomas J. Michalak contributed significantly to developing and testing the Program Matrix at the Columbia University Libraries. Their work is here gratefully acknowledged.

Operational level decisions determine staff assignments, work schedules, processing procedures, material flow, item selection, record control, and the myriad details of providing library service. Decisions concerning processing priorities, procedural alternatives, backlog disposition, circulation control systems, reference service tradeoffs, weeding policy are made at the operational level.

The goal of this essay is to describe a strategic level model of the university library which would support library-wide forecasting, budgeting, and program cost accounting. Such a model, in addition to serving library planning needs, should be of value for communicating priorities, directions, and issues of library costs to university management.

A STRATEGIC LEVEL MODEL OF THE UNIVERSITY LIBRARY

The model proposed here is a two-dimensional array of financial elements and service programs, supported by descriptive submodels. Applying budget or expenditure and income variables, in one dimension the model displays their relationship to each other; in a second dimension it displays their relationship to service programs. Extended to a third dimension, that of organizational components, the model can be used for departmental or functional analysis. At this level it offers opportunities for departmental budgeting, program planning, and cost accounting.

Exhibit 1 depicts a hypothetical one-dimensional array of expense and income variables for the library. It might be seen as a straightforward budget summary or statement of sources and applications of funds by object category. The elements listed as expense items are typical of those which appear in the library budget; e.g., salaries and wages, books and serials, administrative expenses. The income elements may not actually appear in the budget or accounting statements for the library, but are typical revenues or fund sources; e.g., institutional income, endowments, gifts, fines, and fees.

Exhibit 2 presents a similarly illustrative array of financial operating variables and library programs for the same library. It is a summary of sources and applications of funds by program. In this exhibit, the programs are common to most academic research libraries; e.g., reference, circulation, interlibrary loan, acquisitions processing, catalog processing, collection materials, and administration. Some of these are subdivided into two or more components to improve the model's usefulness. Regular circulation, interlibrary loan, and short term course reserve circulation are all circulation control activities, but making materials available and record keeping for these three modes is different enough to merit their separation for managerial purposes. Similarly, cataloging might be thought of as creating access and inventory records, including the in-

UNIVERSITY LIBRARY X

EXPENSES & INCOME

Year 19__

EXPENSES

Professional Salaries	[ ]
Support Salaries	[ ]
Student Wages	[ ]
Fringe Benefits	[ ]
Books	[ ]
Serials	[ ]
Binding	[ ]
Suppl., Equip., Travel, Other	[ ]
Physical Facilities	[ ]
TOTAL	[ ]

INCOME

General Funds	[ ]
Unrestricted Endowment	[ ]
Restricted Endowment	[ ]
Gifts	[ ]
Fines	[ ]
Access Fees	[ ]
Database Search	[ ]
Photocopy, Reprography	[ ]
Other	[ ]
TOTAL	[ ]
NET (EXPENSE)/REVENUE	[ ]

EXHIBIT 1: SOURCES AND APPLICATIONS OF FUNDS

UNIVERSITY LIBRARY X PROGRAM MATRIX YEAR 19___	Reference & Bibliography	Circulation	Reserves	Interlibrary Loan	Collection Development	Materials Acquisitions	Serials Maintenance	Book Preparation	Catalog Production	Catalog Maintenance	Preservation	Collection Materials	Physical Facilities	Administration	TOTAL
EXPENSES															
Professional Salaries															
Support Salaries															
Student Wages															
Fringe Benefits															
Books															
Serials															
Binding															
Suppl.,Equip.,Travel,Other															
Physical Facilities															
TOTAL															
INCOME															
General Funds															
Unrestricted Endowment															
Restricted Endowment															
Gifts															
Fines															
Access Fees															
Database Search															
Photocopy, Reprography															
Other															
TOTAL															
NET (EXP)/REV															

EXHIBIT 2

LIBRARY PROGRAM MATRIX

tellectual work of determining the record content as well as the clerical work of producing cards, filing, correcting, and adding information. But again, the choice is to separate catalog record creation from catalog file maintenance to distinguish two extensive and quite different activities.

Both Exhibit 1, the Budget Summary, and Exhibit 2, the Library Program Matrix, correspond to the strategic decision level. Management control information rests in submodels underlying each of the program categories and financial elements. Operational level decisions, not addressed here, would be supported by detailed fund and cash flow accounting and by detailed procedural models underlying the management control submodels.

The success of translating the Library Program Matrix into a useful model hinges on program definition and financial variable identification. There must be agreement among potential users on a common set of programs and financial elements which will describe library activity adequately for planning and control. A collective definition process applying the experience and needs of individuals representing several university libraries would improve the likelihood of achieving a commonly accepted set of definitions and also enhance the value of the Matrix for interinstitutional comparisons.

If the model is to be general, it must be insulated from institutional differences and even from the bias of organizational variations in program support within a single institution. Emphasis on library instruction or indexing in one branch or departmental library of a multi-library system should not in itself determine the identification of those as separate programs. Generalization should be possible at the strategic planning level represented in the Program Matrix. It may be more difficult at the management control level of submodels governing program implementation, where organizational differences influence staffing arrangements. Generalization is practically impossible at the operating level, as detailed procedures become more significant in the data relationships. At the strategic level, however, the focus is on programs and function common to most academic libraries and independent of administrative arrangements, workflows, and reporting relationships.

FINANCIAL VARIABLES

Addressing first the issues of financial element identification, the model can be as detailed or as simple as appropriate to meet the needs of the research library community and also balance convenience and verisimilitude. The variables selected to describe the model in this paper are at a summary level.

For illustration, salary costs appear in the exhibits as professional, clerical, student, and fringe benefits. Fringe benefits might be separated into three lines in a submodel, one for each category of staff, to accommodate different fringe rates. Student wages might be separated in the Matrix or in a submodel into regular and government supported work-study, with the work-study reimbursement reflected as a revenue component, or as a lower effective wage rate. Distinguishing institutionally supported student employees from work-study students would permit analysis of the impact of reduced government support, or of changes in the reimbursement formula.

Physical space costs are listed as a single line. They could appear as multiple lines or be represented in a submodel as Utilities, Maintenance and Repairs, Cleaning and Custodial, and Security. The single line for administrative expenses also might be separated into at least major components, such as travel, supplies, equipment.

Although sources of income are not necessarily under library control, they are taken into account in the Matrix for completeness and to allow revenue assumptions to be applied to the model. Again, the degree of detail displayed or manipulated depends on user consensus regarding convenience and usefulness. Much of the detail will be more appropriate in submodels. It might be valuable, for example, to be able to simulate capitalization of a portion of endowment income and then evaluate dynamically the impact of reduced current expenditures against future income growth, under different assumptions of endowment pool rate of return, salary and wage growth, and materials inflation.

Principal revenue components include institutional general or unrestricted funds, library restricted funds, library unrestricted funds, private gifts, and government grants. Depending on university and library policy, there may be additional sources of funds. Fines for overdue materials, access fees, interlibrary loan fees, data base reference fees, photocopy and other reprography income, proceeds from the sale of duplicates, cost recovery arrangements with other institutions to provide access or processing services, and publication royalties and reprint fees are some of these additional sources.

The significance of various revenue sources in the library budget will determine their representation at the strategic level. Certain elements may be insignificant enough in most libraries so that they might be summarized as Miscellaneous Fees and analyzed in a submodel. In some cases, the revenue might pass through to the university. The model should indicate this in some way, perhaps as a summary negative income entry.

BUDGETING AND FORECASTING

In the first dimension, that of expenses and income (Exhibit 1), the model can be used as a budgeting or forecasting tool. To this extent, it is similar to the TRADES system developed at Stanford University.[2] Exhibit 3 shows the first dimension of the model as a five-year forecast for the entire library.

UNIVERSITY LIBRARY X
FIVE YEAR FORECAST
Year 19___ - Year 19___

EXPENSES	YEAR 1	YEAR 2	DIFF. YEAR 2-1	YEAR 3	DIFF. YEAR 3-2	YEAR 4	DIFF. YEAR 4-3	YEAR 5	DIFF. YEAR 5-4
Professional Salaries									
Support Salaries									
Student Wages									
Fringe Benefits									
Books									
Serials									
Binding									
Suppl.,Equip.,Travel,Other									
Physical Facilities									
TOTAL									
INCOME									
General Funds									
Unrestricted Endowment									
Restricted Endowment									
Gifts									
Fines									
Access Fees									
Database Search									
Photocopy, Reprography									
Other									
TOTAL									
NET (EXPENSE)/REVENUE									

EXHIBIT 3

FIVE-YEAR FORECAST

Expense and income relationships expressed in financial submodels can be manipulated and displayed to reflect current operations or anticipated levels of activity. The impact of changes in fringe benefits, materials inflation, photocopy charges, restricted fund income, and other variables can be observed under different assumptions at this level.

Used only as a budget summary or forecast, the model is of value primarily for incremental analysis independent of program changes. The effect of massive infusions of book funds on staff expenditures, for example, would depend on program and policy decisions. It is possible to greatly increase book expenditures with no increase in processing staff if the library is tolerant of accumulating backlogs. The same would be true of other major decisions such as establishing a new departmental library, entering a cataloging network, creating a regional interlibrary loan network, and so forth. They can be made without necessarily affecting the budgets of every operating department one might expect, although such decisons would certainly affect program activity in those departments. Just as there is no automatic or simple relationship between book funds and staff expenditures, expenditures for staff in acquisitions and cataloging, reference and circulation, interlibrary loan and collection development, and various combinations of these are undoubtedly related, but in complex ways that elude the generality of a line item budget forecast.

Strategic decisions have far ranging program and budgetary effects which are better addressed for analytical purposes at the program level, the second dimension of the model. Major financial decisions, as well as incremental ones, reflect priorities and affect programs. They should be made and evaluated in the context of these effects, and not as abstract financial transactions.

PROGRAM DEFINITION

The challenge is expanding the model to the second dimension comes in defining a manageable number of programs which will effectively describe all library activities. The quality of the program definitions will determine the value of this facet of the model. Programs identified should reflect library management concern for service and administrative priorities. This suggests some balance among public services, the direct patron contact activities, and technical services, the indirect patron contact activities, with some attention given to administrative services that are essential to general library service quality or ambiance.

Program definitions are subject to interpretation and disagreement. It is important to establish commonly acceptable definitions that will be useful to display the relative magnitude of program activity, to communicate priorities and needs, and to indicate or reflect changes in cost related to policy or procedural changes.

Ultimately, the programs identified should be selected and defined according to what is of greatest interest or value to the library management community. Guidelines for program definition might include uniqueness of procedures; identifiable service-related goals; special qualifications, skills or activities of the staff engaged in the program; and magnitude of resources committed to it. Certain programs might be identified primarily on the basis of their managerial priority, as a way to highlight their importance and monitor their progress, although they might not be particularly costly relative to other programs. These guidelines may be helpful, but the real test will be the rationality and usefulness of the programs identified.

PUBLIC SERVICES, TECHNICAL SERVICES, ADMINISTRATION

Because the principal goal of library activity is user satisfaction, public service programs have typically been the focus of library evaluation and performance analysis in comprehensive library models.[3,4] User perceptions and library responsiveness to user needs are logical areas to give attention if the measure of success is user satisfaction.

However, limiting service measures to direct public contact omits a major part of library activity. Identifying technical services only as a single program obscures much activity that results eventually in user service and represents significant costs. Also, if one is concerned with cost reduction and increased output, technical service areas are particularly susceptible to productivity measurement and productivity improvement. Some reasonable number of identifiable technical service programs should be included for anlaysis and scrutiny.

Administrative programs should be included because they represent major costs, reflect managerial policy, and indirectly affect public service through the physical service environment and staffing of the library.

Several taxonomies have been used to evaluate library services or costs. The service program definitions in Exhibit 4 are based on those in Bommer,[5] and Hamburg,[6] and on an unpublished methodology for financial analysis developed at the Columbia University Libraries.

PROGRAM DEFINITIONS PROBLEMS

Some of the difficulties attendant on program definition can be illustrated by the following examples:

1. Cataloging record creation and catalog maintenance might be succinctly defined as "organizing and describing collections to facilitate access." However, this also applies to indexing and bibliography preparation, two activities more commonly associated with reference service. Indeed, they are here included in the Reference program on grounds that a

EXHIBIT 4

Service Program Definitions

1. **Reference and Bibliography Service:** render assistance in document identification and location; interpret bibliographical records and reference tools; assist in using library materials; answer questions; assist access to materials on order or recently processed.

   Prepare indexes or bibliographies to identify, locate documents, or provide information; assign entry points, prepare entries or annotations; create records, maintain thesauri.

   Provide assistance or instruction in the use of the library, its access tools, collections, services; develop aids for library instruction: lectures, tours, orientation.

2. **Circulation:** provide patron access to materials; create and maintain records of materials on loan or requested; produce transaction notices - recalls, overdues, holds; prepare collection inventory, search for materials as required; fetch and reshelve items; maintain stacks.

3. **Reserves:** provide short-term circulation control services and records; process reserve requests and materials; fetch and reshelve items.

4. **Interlibrary Loan:** conduct borrowing and lending transactions with other libraries; fetch and reshelve materials; maintain records; wrap, ship and receive materials.

5. **Collection Development:** identify, select, evaluate and weed materials; assess user needs; solicit gifts; develop relations with the book trade.

6. **Materials Acquisitions:** search and prepare order requests, create and maintain order and receipt records, e.g. claims, payments, check-in, etc.; maintain serials holdings.

   Includes vendor assignment, invoice processing, receipt and routing of materials, vendor and donor correspondence.

7. **Serials Maintenance:** maintain serial order and receipt records, e.g. claims, payments, check-in, etc.; maintain serials holdings.

8. **Book Preparation:** prepare materials for (non-reserves) use, pocketing, plating, spine marking, ownership stamping.

9. **Catalog Production:** create records organizing and describing collections for intellectual and physical access; maintain quality control via authority work to ensure uniform names and subject headings; perform precataloging searching, original cataloging, and cataloging with copy.

10. **Catalog Maintenance:** file or correct catalogs, shelflists, and authority files in card form or through computer terminals; process transfers, withdrawals, additions, and editorial changes to catalogs.

11. **Preservation:** select and treat items for preservation; prepare serial or monograph volumes for binding, microfilming, photocopying, laminating, or other protective or restorative processing; identify deteriorated or lost materials for replacement; create and maintain control records for items treated.

12. **Collection Materials:** Funds for books, serials, documents, non-print media, binding.

Exhibit 4 (continued)

13. Physical Facilities: space, furnishings, equipment, utilities and maintenance of user study, recreation, and service areas, lecture and meeting rooms, materials storage areas, library staff areas.

14. Administration: provide general administrative support services; allocate resources and determine program priorities; organize services and staffing; prepare budgets, statistics and reports; administer personnel activities, including staff evaluation, training, and general organizational development; maintain liaison and good relations with user groups; coordinate activities among operating units; provide secretarial and other support services - local mail, photocopying, correspondence and report typing, office files, maintenance, supplies.

different type of staff performs indexing and creates bibliographies; the initiative and audience for those activities are different and highly specialized; and they are, in fact, traditionally public service, reference activities. Hence, although catalogers could undoubtedly perform indexing and some catalogers are as specialized as some indexers and bibliographers, the categorization here is based on the detailed performance of the function, its place in the organization of library work, and the traditional definitions of cataloging as technical service and bibliography as public service. In the methodology developed at Columbia, Indexing-Bibliography Preparation was a separately defined program to distinguish it from cataloging and from other types of reference work involving direct public contact. This offers another solution to the dilemma.

2. Circulation is a function common to most libraries, characterized especially by record keeping for control over materials in use. The type or intensity of record keeping, the staffing, and the materials handling procedures for course reserves, interlibrary loan, and regular long term circulation are different. Addressing them separately is likely to be more informative and offer better prospects for managerial control, policy analysis and service improvement. Hence they are separated in the hypothetical model.

3. Preservation costs can be considered part of the book preparation process that makes material available and usable. They can also be considered a cost of collection materials themselves, and in a sense are, as commercial binding expenditures are included in all statutory or professional association reports of materials expenditures. The intellectual tasks of identifying items in need of preservation, and designating the treatment to be given, can be considered adjunct to the collection development process; they determine the continued role in the collection of the item under consideration, much as do selection and weeding. In fact, binding, restoration, microfilming and other activities are not identifiable with any single public or technical service program. In most research libraries, the importance and high cost of preservation argue for its separation as a pro-

gram for monitoring and control rather than subsuming preservation costs under other service programs. For reporting and historical consistency, commercial binding funds are included here in the Collection Materials program, although with misgivings and with the belief that this policy should be rationalized in surveys and standards for library operating data.

4. Serials are quite distinct from monographs in their treatment and processing, after their initial ordering is finished. The continuing costs and unique procedures for handling serials suggest their isolation for program analysis, although there is need for some judgment of how refined the program definition should be. At the simplest level, there is one program: Serials Maintenance—continuing check-in, claiming and payment. However, if all serials-related costs are of interest and to be identified, then serials binding and catalog update might be separated as program components, as well as the initial procedures for acquisitions, claiming, and payment. But Serials Catalog Update and Serials Binding as individual programs would conflict with the programs Catalog Maintenance and Preservation, under which they are now subsumed. The choice must be made, again, according to what is most important to the user of the system or most practical for associating costs and activities. Here, the decision is to identify Serials Maintenance only, and leave programs identified as Serials Acquisition, Serials Cataloging, and Serials Binding for submodel development.

5. Physical facilities present special problems of program definition. They are at once public service costs, technical service costs, and administrative overhead. They are capital costs and current expenses. Finally, they do not appear at all in most university library budgets except perhaps for minor improvements and repairs. For convenience, all physical plant costs are defined here as Physical Facilities, with building area, furnishings, maintenance, and other refinements left for submodel representation to the degree desirable. Submodel development would be especially valuable to support decisions on extended hours of access, physical location of specific programs, remodeling, or new construction.

In applying the model to actual libraries, physical facilities costs may be the area of greatest difficulty, based on the likely unavailability of the data in some institutions, and on differences in accounting practices which would affect values from institution to institution. To the extent that institutional analysis is available, it should be adapted to a submodel. If direct program cost assignment cannot be made or is overly refined, it might ultimately be best to treat physical facilities as a separate program, which is the case in this presentation. Alternatively, these costs might be defined as overhead to be distributed among programs according to some formula or other. This would be consistent with the proposal that libraries use a commercial style markup for costing certain services.[7]

6. Other administrative support programs are tempting prospects for

analysis because of their cost, their immediate or ultimate impact on public service, and their interest in the library profession. These include systems development and maintenance, and staff training and development. They are here subsumed in the program Administration, although as with physical facilities, their costs might be distributed by formula, treated as overhead, or refined in the submodel.

PROGRAM SUBMODELS

Although financial and program variables are ultimately related, each set in the proposed model is intended to be manipulated independently through submodels to simplify the initial implementation. Manipulation of financial variables is a familiar part of fiscal planning and budgeting. The result, as in Exhibit 1, is a list of elements resulting in equilibrium, a surplus, or a deficit.

In a similar way, program submodels are intended to represent program activity and expenditure relationships and take into account service assumptions and policy decisions. The goal here is not a fully integrated operational level model of the university library. Rather, it is a series of independent models designed to give a realistic character to the impact of financial and service decisions. Some of them might perhaps be related even in an initial implementation.

Constrained network analysis and linear programming have been used successfully in models of the acquisitions, cataloging, and interlibrary loan functions.[8] Such mathematical expressions can be used to describe rigorously the financial and program relationships in the proposed model. Alternatively, decisions can be applied to the model in a qualitative manner reflecting the individual library manager's experience, judgment, and use of operating data. Either way, or using some combination of these, a programmatic display of the results will allow comparative evaluation of the effects of the decisions, assumptions, and policies underlying the changes.

Depending on the extent of detail and operational level information desired in the submodels, they can be developed for general application or refined to a high degree for specific libraries. For example, Materials Acquisitions includes searching, to determine whether the item is already held and also to verify the order information; vendor assignment and order verification; order review and claim preparation for materials not received; invoice processing and payment; gift solicitation; and exchange solicitation. These are performed in various libraries by different levels of staff in different organizational units, according to the size and structure of the library. Further, the method of acquisitions—gift, exchange, approval, blanket order—will affect the procedure and cost of processing, as will the tolerance of delays and backlogs.

For purposes of modeling at the strategic and management control level, the submodels should represent aggregate procedures to the extent possible. Hence, the submodel would address gross level staffing to handle a certain volume of order requests, item receipts, and invoices processed under certain service conditions determined by policy or assumption. More detailed procedural and workflow submodels would be left to an operational level model.

DEPARTMENT LEVEL PROGRAM MATRIX

The proposed model as outlined so far describes the entire library system. The Program Matrix may be applied in a third dimension at the departmental or functional level to describe suborganizational activity. This is depicted in Exhibit 5.

At this level, the Matrix is amenable to cost accounting and to data collection for the aggregate Matrix. An additional line is necessary to allow for central technical services support where public service departments have little or no technical service responsibilities. Completion of this line would require accounting for program expenditures in central departments and then distributing those costs by some means to client departments. Volumes or titles processed might be the basis for certain cost distributions. Other measures might be used for distributing centrally provided administrative, physical facilities, or other costs.

This is the level at which institution specific arrangements become visible in any effort to describe submodels mathematically or algorithmically. Implementation at this level will be fruitful only for individual libraries because of the variation in procedures among libraries. The Departmental Program Matrix is offered here to be used qualitatively or as a means to support higher level analysis.

DEPARTMENT LEVEL APPLICATIONS

Departmental program costs for evaluative or comparative purposes are one result of the more detailed level Matrix completion. Budget planning and control are further applications. Finally, with an output measure for certain programs, unit costing is possible at the department level. This might be useful in charging for services or in program planning, and of course, again for interdepartmental or interinstitutional cost comparisons.

Unit costing and chargeback analysis would also be available at the aggregate level based on library-wide output measures. Total cataloging or acquisitions output in records, volumes, or titles is readily available through computer based technical processing systems. Unit costing for

UNIVERSITY LIBRARY X
DEPARTMENT 1
PROGRAM MATRIX

Year 19___

EXPENSES	Reference & Bibliography	Circulation	Reserves	Interlibrary Loan	Collection Development	Materials Acquisitions	Serials Maintenance	Book Preparation	Catalog Production	Catalog Maintenance	Preservation	Collection Materials	Physical Facilities	Administration	TOTAL
Professional Salaries															
Support Salaries															
Student Wages															
Fringe Benefits															
Books															
Serials															
Binding															
Suppl., Equip., Travel, Ot															
Physical Facilities															
Central Tech. Services															
TOT															

INCOME
- General Funds
- Unrestricted Endowment
- Restricted Endowment
- Gifts
- Fines
- Access Fees
- Database Search
- Photocopy, Reprography
- Other

TOT

NET (EXPENSE)/REVENUE

UNIVERSITY LIBRARY X
DEPARTMENT 2
PROGRAM MATRIX

Year 19___

EXPENSES
- Professional Salaries
- Support Salaries
- Student Wages
- Fringe Benefits
- Books
- Serials
- Binding
- Suppl., Equip., Travel, Ot
- Physical Facilities
- Central Tech. Services

TOT

INCOME
- General Funds
- Unrestricted Endowment
- Restricted Endowment

UNIVERSITY LIBRARY X
DEPARTMENT 3
PROGRAM MATRIX

Year 19___

EXPENSES
- Professional Salaries
- Support Salaries
- Student Wages
- Fringe Benefits
- Books
- Serials

EXHIBIT 5

DEPARTMENTAL PROGRAM MATRIX

the library might be built into the general Library Program Matrix as an additional bottom line in the expense category.

DATA COLLECTION

Whether data collection takes place through the Departmental Program Matrix or is applied directly to the Library Progam Matrix, some mechanism is necessary to gather actual expenditure, revenue, and program related cost information and use it in the model. Basic revenue and expense data should be available from institutional budget or accounting systems, with a few exceptions for aspects of physical facilities. Financial submodel development and data collection will depend to some extent on assistance from university administration. Certain of the data itself and some of the relationships are not known within the library.

Program related financial information may be more difficult to acquire. Some form of staff survey is necessary to identify time devoted to program activities. The time must then be translated into dollars according to the level of staff and salaries paid per unit of time. Techniques for accomplishing this are well established in management and library administration literature. With careful design and implementation, sufficiently accurate data can be gathered via activity diaries or sample surveys. Other than personnel costs are important and grow increasingly so as communications and computer equipment, information utility services, and new published tools become essential to the library's work. The degree of refinement of the data collection methodology will determine its cost, and is ultimately a matter of balancing that cost against the perceived value of the results.

Data gathering in some organizational units is less costly than in others, depending on the degree of program specialization practiced in the unit. Departments dedicated to reference, interlibrary loan, circulation, and acquisitions are obvious cases in which the entire cost can be assigned to one program without a detailed survey. However, the process should be sensitive to flexibility in staff assignments. For example, the circulation department that devotes staff time during slack periods to filing in the catalog is contributing to Catalog Maintenance. Similarly, the cataloging department's responsibilities might include Catalog Maintenance as well as Production.

Relatively small, self sustaining branch libraries are likely to be the costliest data collection environment, and most subject to error as the same staff might engage in a multitude of program activities from pre-order searching through book plating and pocketing to checking-in serials and addressing overdue notices. It is probable that with a higher degree of centralization and specialization, the data gathering costs will be lower and the results more accurate.

FINAL COMMENTS

In considering the development of a strategic information model, one must not overlook the essential relationship of financial, policy and procedural decisions.[9] Financial decisions in the absence of policy considerations can result in unpredictable or uncontrollable and possibly detrimental effects on policy or operations. A strategic model independent of operating information may be interesting in its indication of the realities of program costs, valuable in its reflection of priorities as measured in financial terms, and useful for general discussion with university administration. However, it will not, in itself yield program savings, cost reductions, productivity improvements, or improved service. It may point the way by revealing discrepant or excessive costs, or costs that appear inconsistent with prescribed policy. Nevertheless, to translate these observations into tangible improvements would require investigation at the control or operational level. The discovery that acquisitions cost are higher for one library than for another will neither explain nor automatically reduce the difference. The reasons for the differences lie in the detail underlying staff expenditures and even staff distribution among professional, support and student staff; they are in the details of the type of materials being ordered, the nature of tools used in preparing orders, the sources of the materials, and the specific work procedures. It is these details which ultimately must change if improvement is sought.

It should also be noted that financial modeling of the research library in a university context presents some special problems. Some expenditure elements which appear in the university budget may not be part of the library budget, e.g., utilities, housekeeping, plant capital. Other revenue components may not be applicable and are not under librarian control, e.g., indirect cost recovery, endowment payout, tuition. The library's budget is in most cases "received" from the university. It is subject to growth and decline assumptions, but not necessarily subject to actual control or manipulation—it is not ultimately determined by the librarian.

In some respects this simplifies model building because certain complexities are lacking and perhaps need not be addressed to describe effectively library operating expenditures. On the other hand, if the model is to be useful in relating library finances to policy decisions, the missing elements must be accounted for, sources of income accommodated, and program level relationships defined.

Finally, it is not uncommon for the university library to be seen by university administrators as a central cost almost independent of teaching and research programs. The library's budget, therefore, is not always perceived or developed as subject to the direct impact of changes in academic programs, student or faculty population, or the sources of revenue underlying university activities—tuition, sponsored research, academic program grants, university gifts and endowment income. This problem of university management perceptions of the library is serious if these perceptions interfere with rational dialogue between university library managers and university budget managers. If library activities and their relationship to academic programs are not understood and are seen primarily as a nebulous component of the research or teaching process, it is virtually impossible for the librarian to justify legitimate incremental needs except as solutions to crises. In this case, the library is condemned to marginal growth and internal resource shifts to meet ever more demanding program requirements. To the extent that a financial planning model can strengthen the relationship between the library and the university, both interests are well served in developing one.

NOTES

1. R. W. Bommer, R. W. Chorba, and W. Grattide, *Decision Support Systems for the Management of Academic Libraries*, Potsdam, N.Y., The School of Management, Clarkson College of Technology, 1980 (Draft).
2. Nathan Dickmeyer, David S. P. Hopkins, and William F. Massy, "TRADES: A Model for Interactive Financial Planning", in *Business Officer*, March, 1978, p. 22-27.
3. Bommer, *Decision Support Systems*.
4. Morris Hamburg, et al., *Library planning and decision making systems*. Cambridge, Mass., MIT Press, 1974.
5. Bommer, *Decision Support Systems*, p. 24.
6. Hamburg, *Library planning*, p. 60.
7. Harvey Marron. "On Costing Information Services", in American Society for Information Science. Annual Meeting, 32nd, San Francisco, California, October 1-4, 1969. *Proceedings. 6.* (Westport, Connecticut: Greenwood Publishing Company, 1969), p. 515-520.
8. Diane Davis Cole, *Mathematical Models in Library Management: Planning, Analysis, and Cost Assessment*. Dissertation, University of Texas at Austin, May, 1976.
9. NACUBO, "Costing for Policy Analysis", Washington, D.C., 1980, p. 3.

Academic Library Decision Support Systems

Michael Bommer
Ronald Chorba

EMERGING TRENDS

The increasing use of sophisticated electronic systems is transforming the way academic libraries collect, store and transfer human knowledge. From automated cataloging and circulation to selected dissemination of information services, these support systems represent a wealth of untapped information for use in the planning and management of library resources and services.

At the same time the administration of the academic institution is also collection and processing a wealth of relevent information. Included are such elements as databanks on text book usage, course descriptions, and faculty assignments; information on faculty-generated research proposals, grant awards, publications and papers; and information on enrollment patterns, new programs, changes in existing ones and new pedagogical trends.

From outside the institution information on trends in the production of knowledge and societal priorities represents a further source of information germane to library planning and management.

Future prospects are that library management will continue to be faced with providing increased access to a volume of knowledge which is expanding at a dramatic rate. Rising inflationary costs for providing materials and services, coupled with increasing and more sophisticated demands by users, further intensify the situation. At this same time, academic institutional financial and personnel resources are becoming severely constrained and resource allocation for the library is in competition with other institutional activities and operations. Gore (1975 and 1976) predicts that further growth of the local library will not be the solution to information problems and suggests the prospect of zero growth libraries. Schmidt (1975) documents the existence of a declining acquisi-

---

Michael Bommer is affiliated with the School of Management, Clarkson College, Potsdam, NY 13676. Mr. Chorba is also in the School of Management and serves as an Associate Professor.

This paper is based upon research funded by a grant from the National Science Foundation, Division of Information Science and Technology (IST 78-12093).

tion rate among research libraries at a time of an increasing rate of knowledge output.

CHALLENGES AND OPPORTUNITIES

To meet this challenge of providing patrons with increased access to a knowledge base that is growing at an alarming rate, it is vital that the library's resources, human, material and financial, be utilized in the most effective and efficient manner. In a study conducted by Booz, Allen and Hamilton, Inc. (1980), four major areas were targeted for managerial improvement in the 1980s. These areas were identified as the strategic areas which will yield the greatest degree of benefits or output as a result of improvements in management design and action. These areas are depicted in Figure 1.

Recently, much attention has been focused on office support cost reductions. New advances in equipment design, especially those utilizing computer capabilities, are increasing the productivity of secretarial staff. While these advances are offering improvements in the productivity of secretarial staff, significant future increases in the office support area are not forecasted to occur in the same magnitude as increases in the other areas. Future increases in productivity in the office area are expected to be modest in comparison to opportunities in other areas because of the current high state of technology of office equipment and the disproportionately smaller amount of expenditures for and in support of office staff as compared with professional and managerial staff. In contrast the potential gains from improvements in productivity and decision making with regard to the professional and managerial staff are enormous.

New forms of organizational design will emerge which will develop and utilize human resources more effectively at all levels. The classic pyramid structure of early organizations reflects earlier social values and a personnel-based technology. Changes in social values, improvements in technology and increases in personal skills have combined with changes in client needs to promote new organizational forms. As a result, organizations have begun to embrace more cooperative endeavors with decision-making and authority more decentralized and moved to lower levels. The pyramid structure became more rectangular in shape. New forms will continue to evolve to cope with changing values and to increase the effectiveness of human resources at all levels. In future organizations, work loads will be more balanced, work support services more accessible, and there will be greater emphasis on the needs and merits on individual employees.

The productivity of the professional staff will be enhanced through the application of advances in computer and communications technology, and through better utilization of their own time. The trends represented by computer-aided bibliographic searches and computerized cataloging will continue to improve productivity. At the same time professionals will need to learn more about time management. Here both technology and training have a role to play: technology by providing more efficient task support; and training by improving the individual's capacity to perform more effectively.

Finally, improved decision making and planning will be required to utilize and allocate the library's resources in the most efficient and effective manner. The library manager must be able to identify problems, needs, and trends, and then must respond with decisions and programs which direct resources appropriately to best support the overall objectives of the institution. Sound decision making and planning, however, require appropriate management information and models. Much of this information is available from existing databases, as a by-product of automated or computerized operating systems or can be captured from various sources. A number of studies have been conducted and models developed for aiding managerial decision making and planning. In the next decade, comprehensive decision support systems will be developed which combine information and modeling, tailored to the unique needs and style of individual managers. These systems will significantly improve the effectiveness of library managers in making decisions and plans.

All four areas are important to the improvement of library effec-

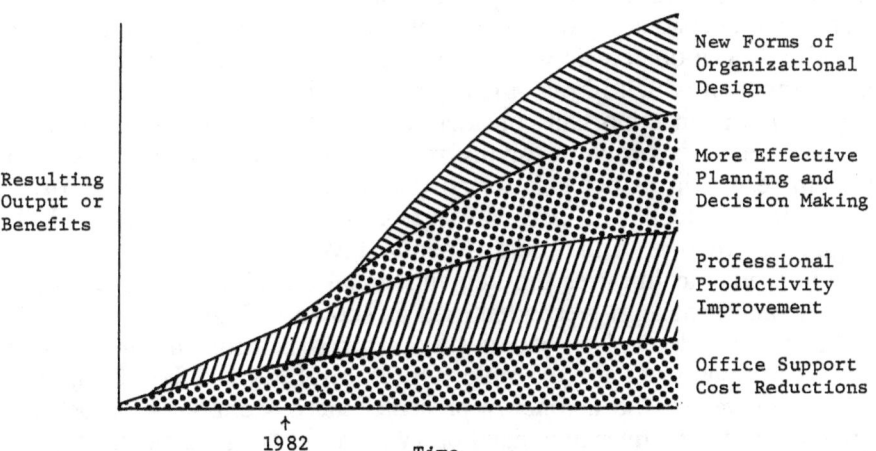

Figure 1

Resulting Output or Benefits Over Time as a Function of Management Evolution

(Adapted from Booz, Allen & Hamilton, Inc. Study (1980)).

tiveness in the next decade: office support cost reduction; new forms of organizational design; professional productivity improvement; and more effective planning and decision making. This paper, however, focuses primarily on one of these areas—more effective planning and decision making. In particular, a framework is explored for designing a decision support system DSS for library management.

DIMENSIONS OF DECISION MAKING

Critical to the development of a decision support system is the identification of a link between the decision-making process and the information elements required to support the decision process. Specification of the information elements to be included in the support system is a function of the types of decisions to be made and the decision process employed by the manager. Lucas (1974) states that identification of the "type of decision involved and the informational requirements for each decision type are essential in the design or analysis of an information system." Ackoff (1967) believes that for managers to know what information is needed, they must be aware of each type of decision as well as have an adequate model for each decision.

As a first step in identifying informational needs, the decision process for academic libraries needs to be analyzed and delineated. The dimensions of the framework include (1) key functional areas, (2) managerial level, (3) degree of structure, and (4) decision stage. These dimensions provide a basis for identifying informational requirements within the decision process for designing an overall decision support system.

One taxonomy for classifying decisions is according to key library functions. Goals and objectives for several academic libraries were surveyed and analyzed to identify these key functional areas. Those objectives which were most frequently cited and those judged to involve significant decisions regarding current and future library directions were identified. The objectives which emerged were classified in reference to the manner in which library managers view library services and operations. This is an important consideration as incompatibility between the decision-maker's problem-solving mode and the format of the support system results in its not being used (Churchman and Schainblatt 1975). To be truly effective, a decision support system should mesh with the cognitive structure of the users (Keen and Morton 1978).

For academic libraries the key functional decision areas (in no particular rank ordering) were identified as shown in Figure 2.

Many other logical taxonomies exist for structuring library services and operations (see, for example, Orr et al. 1968 and Hamburg et al. 1974). However, the taxonomy presented here seems to be most congruent with the manner in which library managers organize their decision

Figure 2

Key Functional Decision Areas

1. Collection Development
2. Technical Services
3. Reference and Bibliography Service
4. Collection Access
5. Access by Interlibrary Loan
6. Staff Development
7. Physical Facilities
8. Planning, Funding & Information Systems

process, as evidenced by articulated statements of objectives and interviews with selected library managers.

A second dimension of classification for decisions is borrowed from Anthony (1975) and distinguishes decisions made at different organizational levels as illustrated in Figure 3. Decisions in strategic planning relate to selecting objectives, objective priorities, changes in objectives, and resource selection. Management control decisions involve resource allocations within the context of policies and objectives developed in the strategic planning process. Resource allocation decisions involve program development, staffing, levels, funding levels, tradeoff resolution, etc., with respect to appropriate objectives and goals. Operational control decisions assure that specific tasks are performed in an effective and efficient manner. While these categories are not exclusive and overlap exists, they provide useful guidelines for analyzing differing information needs. This study focuses primarily on the strategic planning and management control levels of decision. In particular, it addresses decisions relating to the planning and resource allocation activities.

Another useful dimension for classifying decisions is the degree of structure inherent in the decisions to be made (Simon 1960). Decisions are classified as structured or unstructured, depending upon the degree to which the decision process can be described in detail. Decisions are unstructured because of lack of knowledge, need for value judgment, complexity of the problem, uniqueness of the problem, etc. The distinction between structured and unstructured decisions is not always precise; in fact, decisions more generally lie on a continuum between these two extremes. Nonetheless, this classification scheme is helpful in designing the information support system.

An example of how decisions might be categorized according to the dimensions of degree of structure and decision level is shown in Figure 4.

Figure 3

Decision Levels

Level	Example
1. Strategic Planning	Setting objectives, negotiating interlibrary agreements, adopting major technological innovations, expanding facilities.
2. Management Control	Allocating funds among subject areas, identifying staff development needs, assessing program performance with respect to strategic objectives, determining hours of library service, developing weeding policy, purchasing equipment and services, setting standards for operations.
3. Operational Control	Monitoring daily operations and activities with respect to standards, corrective actions, scheduling, response to complaints, coordinating special requests and projects. Decisions made in performing cataloging, shelving, acquisitions, weeding, circulation, reference, etc.

Figure 4

Decision Classification

Degree of Structure	Decision Level		
	Operational Control	Management Control	Strategic Planning
Structured	Control of New Acquisitions	Staffing of Circulation Desk	Policy on Level of Cataloging
Unstructured	On-line Bibliographic Search Procedure	Allocating Funds to Subject Areas	Collection Development Goals

In the past, most management information systems have been designed to support the more structured decisions, which are routine and repetitive, at the lower decision levels for which definite procedures can be applied. Recently, as a result of advances in technology and increased knowledge of the decision maker, impressive strides have been made in industry to develop decision support systems to assist managers in less structured decision-making situations (Keen and Moreton 1978). In the library environment many, if not most of the decisions, however, are of the less structured nature. To date, precious few applications of information support systems to decisions in the library are in evidence (Bommer 1975 and DeGennaro 1978).

Finally, a fourth dimension of decision making is the distinction between various stages in the decision-making process itself. The most generally accepted view of these stages is given by Simon (1965) and is illustrated in Figure 5.

Library Managers can think of their jobs as being composed of many decision-making tasks, each characterized along the four dimensions: function, level, structure, and stage. The support requirements of any such decision task are dependent on these four attributes. Characteristics of data reported to management such as accuracy, timeliness, source, scope, detail, format, and currency must be compatible with the dimensional attributes. The use of mathematical models, statistical tools, and the body of research findings about effective library operations must also be invoked with the dimensional attributes in mind in libraries.

DECISION TASKS AND INFORMATION NEEDS

Analysis of the goals and objectives of various academic libraries was used to identify functional/areas and key decision tasks within each area. The elements used in identifying functional areas were the goals and objective statements, the library manager's views of library services and operations and the organizational level of the areas. Supplementary personal interviews resulted in a high degree of correspondence on the key decision tasks, although the importance of each varies according to the characteristics and needs of each library. In addition, a review of the

Figure 5

Stages of Decision Making

Stage	Example
Intelligence: Searching for Problems and Opportunities	Complaints, identifying documents which circulate infrequently, measuring adequacy of collection for specific programs, forecasting future needs, identifying potentially useful technological innovations, comparing performance to expectations
Design: Defining and Analyzing Alternative Actions	Data gathering, modeling, and parameter estimation to further understand problem structure, identifying contributing factors, creative generation of possible solutions, discovery of relationships between variables
Choice: Selecting and Implementing a Course of Action	Forecasting implications of alternative actions, evaluating outcomes, dealing with behavioral and technical problems in implementation

literature helped to define more closely the key decision tasks, and the decision models and performance measures relevant to each task. A list of these decision tasks and selected performance measures appears as Figure 6.

INFORMATION SYSTEM EVOLUTION

A decision support system (DSS) can be viewed as a natural progression from an electronic data processing system (EDP) and a management information system (MIS) as depicted in Figure 7.

In stage I, the computer was primarily used as a data processor for transactions and record keeping. Clerical activities were automated with the principal benefit being that data collection and tabulation was performed faster and more efficiently. In stage II, data were converted to information for management use. This was the era of MIS in which standardized reports were provided to support the more routine, repetitive, structured decisions. In stage III, the process is extended to provide information and models which support specific decisions processes. These systems will be designed to conform to the unique style and needs of a manager and arriving at the solution of all problems. The man-machine (manager-computer) system will operate interactively to provide a high degree of synergism in the decision-making and planning process.

In general, the recurring criticism of management information systems is that they contribute little to the really important decisions of upper-management and even at middle-management levels (see, for example, DeGennaro 1978).

The operations research and the systems approach to a decision problem are used to discover and exploit the underlying problem structure. These methods usually require considerable investment of time and money for developing a formal decision model. Many problems, however, are difficult to structure without ignoring important qualitative features. To date, operations and systems research models have been successful only in dealing with the more structured, routine, repetitive problems of which definite procedures can be applied (see Bommer 1975). Thus, many of the important, unstructured decisions must be made without reliance on formalized models and tools.

The quality of decision making in academic libraries depends in large part upon the availability and timeliness of appropriate management information. Information, however, is not the sole component for good decision making and planning. Experience and judgment brought to the problem by the decision maker are also critical ingredients. Ackoff (1967) discusses the need for managers to develop an adequate mental model of a decision problem. Mintzberg (1973) found that managers collect and piece various scraps of information until patterns emerge in their

Figure 6

Decision Tasks

Key Functional Objective Area	Strategic Planning Decisions	Management Decisions	Performance or Effectiveness Measure
Collection Development	Determining Collection Development Goals	Allocation of Funds to Subject Areas Funds Allocated for Books and Serials Types of Books and Serials to be Acquired Degree of Duplication Weeding Policy and Procedures Current/Retrospective Acquisitions Replacement of Lost, Damaged, or Worn Documents Selection Tools Staffing Level for Selection Activities	% Held of Sample Bibliographies Patron Complaints # Reserves for Books Circulation/Subject Area/Document Circulation/User Group Citation Distribution Analysis Selection Cost/Document Minimum Standards Ratio of Documents Selected/Documents Published Document Retrieval Time for Local/ILL Percent Demands Satisfied
Technical Services	Level of Cataloging Timeliness and Cost Efficiency of Document Processing	Acquisition Process Cataloging Data Source Type of Public Bibliographic Record Maintenance of the Public Bibliographic Record Physical Preparation and Maintenance of Documents	Request-Receipt Time Receipt-Shelf Time Cost/Document Processed Entry Points in Catalog per Document Patron Complaints Public Service Staff Complaints

Figure 6
(continued)
Decision Tasks

Key Functional Objective Area	Strategic Planning Decisions	Management Decisions	Performance or Effectiveness Measure

Reference and Bibliographic Service	Level, Coverage, and Quality of Reference Assistance
	Level, Comprehensiveness and Quality of Document Identification Service
	Ready Reference Service
	Formal Library Use Programs
		Manual Literature Searches
		Computerized Literature Searches
		Selected Dissemination of Information Service (SDI)
		Public Relations
			Bibliographies Prepared
			Searches Conducted
			Search Time
			Percent Relevant Citations Obtained
			Patrons Served
			Cost per Search
			Cost per Relevant Citation
			Sample Recall Ratio
			Response Time
			Relevant Bibliographies Services/Subject Area
			Number Served by SDI
			Requests per SDI
			Reference Questions Received
			  Directional
			  Informational
			  Reference
			% Questions Answered
			Cost/Question
			Test Score for Sample Questions
			% Time Staff Providing Reference Services
			% Telephone Requests
			Number Patron Orientation Programs
			Number Patrons Contacted
			Number of Class Presentations
			Complaints

Figure 6
(continued)
Decision Tasks

Key Functional Objective Area	Strategic Planning Decisions	Management Decisions	Performance or Effectiveness Measure
Collection Access	Ease of Access to Collection	Hours of Library Service Arrangement and Location of Collection Level of Collection Security Reshelving and Shelfreading Activities Circulation Control Policy and Procedures Quantity and Type of A-V Equipment Reserve Collection Policies and Procedures	Reshelving Time % Documents Misshelved % Requests in Remote Storage Storage Cost/Document % Documents Lost Half Life/Periodical Subject Area % Documents in Correct Location User Access Time Document Retrieval Time % Demands Satisfied Number of Patrons Number of User Hours % Collection in Open Stacks Circulation/User Group Circulation Cost/Documents Circulated Circulation/Document in Open Stacks Circulation/Document in Closed Stacks
Access by Interlibrary Loan	Interlibrary Loan Cooperative Arrangements	Accessing Documents Held by Other Libraries Supplying Documents to Other Institutions	Retrieval Time % Documents Obtained Cost Per Document Number of Documents Borrowed
Physical Facilities	Quality and Adequacy of User Area and Furnishings	Allocation of Area Number and Type of User Furnishings	Number of Users User Hours Seating/Student Staff Area/Staff Member Density of Document Storage

65

Figure 6
(continued)
Decision Tasks

Key Functional Objective Area	Strategic Planning Decisions	Management Decisions	Performance or Effectiveness Measure
Staff Development	Staff Development Commitment	Identification of Staff Development Needs Type of Programs Sponsored	Staff Turnover Quality of Service Feedback Productivity Papers Presented Seminars Presented Participants/Program Professional Memberships Professional Meetings
Library Planning and Management	Setting Goals and Objectives Library Planning Management Style and Organizational Structure	Acquiring Financial Support Resource Allocation and Control Program and Service Development Program Performance Assessment Data Collection and Information System	Impact Measures Funds Generated Proposals Written Friends of Library Meetings Attended

Figure 7

Information System Progression

	DSS	
	MIS	
EDP		
Stage I	Stage II	Stage III
Processing Data	Producing Information Reports	Synergistic Decision Making
Collection, Tabulation and Aggregation	Standardized Formats	Management and Computer Interaction

⎯⎯⎯⎯⎯⎯⎯⎯⎯⎯⎯⎯⎯⎯⎯⎯⎯⎯⎯⎯⎯⎯⎯⎯→

Computer Use in Decision Making

mind. These patterns combine to form mental models which describe various aspects of a problem. What would appear to be needed, then, is a decision support system which assists the manager in developing these models. Such a system would extend the powers of the decision maker in dealing with these unstructured problems and at the same time should be tailored to the cognitive style of the decision maker.

DECISION SUPPORT SYSTEMS

Recently, a new information systems technology has emerged that has been identified as Decision Support Systems (DSS). Unlike traditional management information systems and operations research techniques, decision support systems rely on the decision maker's insights and judgment at all stages of problem solving—from problem formulation to choosing the relevant data to work with, to picking the approach to be used in generating solutions, and to evaluating the solutions presented to the decision maker (see Edelman 1977). Decision support systems help the manager improve the quality of decisions by providing more insight into all phases of the problem-solving process. Decision support systems extend the range and problem-solving capabilities of managers, especially in dealing with less structured situations.

The provision of decision support capabilities would therefore need to conform to the behavioral needs of managers. Mintzberg (1973) observed that managers carry models and plans in their heads, favor current information over routine reports, and prefer to develop their own information networks. Further, decision making is an iterative process in which answers to one question often lead to another question. A decision support system which is tailored to individual managerial needs and which allows managers to extend their particular decision-making approach would appear to be of significant value.

A few decision support systems are in operation in the business sector (see Carlson 1977 for a report on some applications). By and large, these systems provide for a wide selection of spontaneous as well as scheduled report formats and graphic capabilities. They are interactive, allowing a decision maker to pose and repose questions on a real time basis. The systems provide various capabilities (models and statistical techniques) for analyzing and evaluating data. These systems can access narrative and statistical sets of data which reside in a centralized database and the decision maker (user) has complete control over reports generated by the system.

Figure 8 depicts a conceptual structure of a library decision support system. In this scheme. the Decision Maker Subsystem is comprised of the decision maker, an interactive terminal and screen as well as a command language capability. The Subsystem is comprised of data sources from transactions within the library, within the academic institution as well as data sources external to the institution. The Decision Models Subsystem is comprised of data analysis programs for tabulating and presenting data in various modes and formats, standard modeling programs such as regression analysis, time series analysis, etc., as well as specially developed models to support decisions at various managerial levels.

SUMMARY AND CONCLUSIONS

Library managers, to make effective plans and decisions, require timely access to relevant information and appropriate tools for information analysis. Managers, however, differ in their requirements for information type, content, and form. Educational backgrounds, experiences, personalities, values, perceptions, etc., all affect the manner in which different managers execute their responsibilities. The decision-making process is often informal, with managers collecting and piecing together information until patterns or mental models emerge, using a trial-and-error sequential exploration approach. The experience and judgment of the manager can then be applied to develop effective alternatives and solutions. Highly structured information systems are not helpful in meeting these diverse needs required by differences in the cognitive style and mode of operations of different managers.

The types of decisions faced by library managers also vary widely along a number of dimensions. Some decisions are highly structured while others are quite unstructured. The degree of structure of a decision depends upon the degree of complexity of the decision and the degree to which salient factors can be identified, measured, and related in a

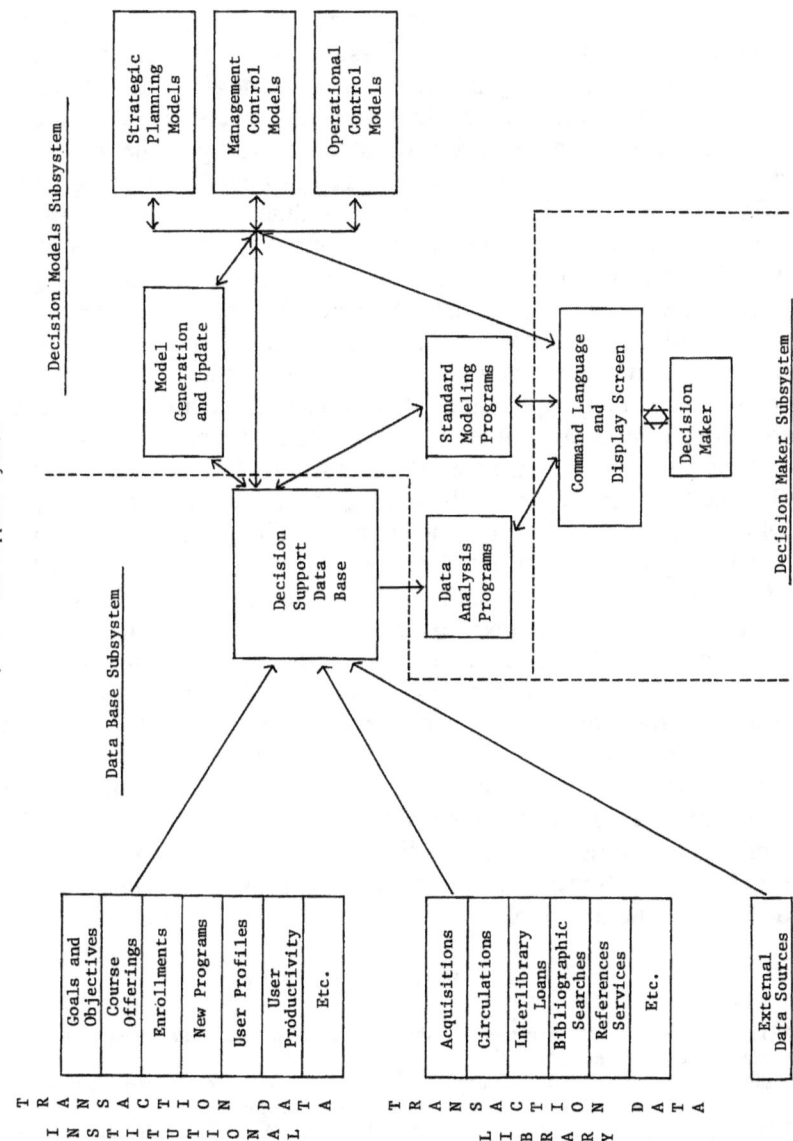

Figure 8
Conceptual Structure of
Library Decision Support System

coherent fashion. Decision types also vary according to the functional area in which they apply within the organization. Functional areas for libraries might be defined in terms of collection development, technical services, reference and bibliographic service, etc. The level of decision making in an organization further serves to define and describe the decision process. A convenient classification of decisions based upon organizational hierarchy is according to strategic planning, management control, and operational control decision levels. Finally, the decision-making process can be further defined according to the various stages of decision making. Three distinct stages of decision making can be identified according to involvement in intelligence (searching for problems and opportunities), design (defining and analyzing alternative actions), and choice (selecting and implementing a course of action). Again, traditional information systems are not effective in supporting decision making in many of these categories, especially the less structured problems, problems at the management and strategic planning level, and decisions at the intelligence and design stages. Decision in these areas represent some of the more important problems facing library management today.

What is needed is a support system which is sufficiently robust and flexible to aid managers with varying cognitive styles in making decisions which vary widely in type and makeup. The development of a Decision Support System (DSS) for library managers would seem to satisfy many of these diverse needs. DSS utilizes the recent advances in computer technology to assist and extend the decision-making capabilities of management. DSS recognizes the unique decision-making styles and preferences of different managers and is designed with sufficient flexibility to accomodate these varying needs. This flexibility in design allows different managers to process and retrieve different information according to different dimensions, formats and levels of detail. Classification and graphical analysis comparisons allow contrasts of one information element to another and according to different time periods to observe trends and relationships. The emphasis is thus on *process* rather than product, allowing a flexible approach to decision-making.

BIBLIOGRAPHY

Ackoff, Russell L. "Management Misinformation Systems." *Management Science*, vol. 14, December 1967, pp. 147-156.

Anthony, R. N. *Planning and Control Systems: A Framework for Analysis.* Cambridge, MA: Harvard University Graduate School of Business Administration, 1975.

Bommer, Michael. "Operations Research in Libraries: A Critical Assessment." *Journal of the American Society for Information Science*, vol. 26, May-June 1975, pp. 137-139.

Booz, Allen and Hamilton. *The Strategic Impact of Information Technology in the 1980s.* A special presentation. New York, 1980.

Carlson, Eric D., ed. "Proceedings of a Conference on Decision Support Systems." *Data Base*, vol. 8, Winter 1977, the issue.

Churchman, C. West and Schainblatt, A. H. "The Researcher and the Manager: A Dialectic of Implementation." *Management Science*, vol. 11, no. 4, 1975.

DeGennaro, Richard. "Library Administrators and New Management Systems." *Library Journal*, vol. 103, December 15, 1978, pp. 2477-2482.

Edelman, Franz. "They Went Thataway." *Interfaces*, vol. 7, May 1977, pp. 39-43.

Gore, Daniel, ed. *Farewell to Alexandria: Solutions to Space, Growth, and Performance Problems of Libraries*. Westport, CT: Greenwood Press, 1976.

Gore, Daniel. "Let them Eat Cake While Reading Catalog Cards: An Essay on the Availability Problem." Library Journal, vol. 100, January 15, 1975, pp. 93-98.

Hamburg, Morris, Clelland, Richard, Bommer, Michael, Ramist, Leonard and Whitfield, Ronald. *Library Planning and Decision-Making Systems*. Cambridge, MA: M.I.T. Press, 1974.

Keen, P. G. W. and Morton, Michael S. Scott. *Decision Support Systems: An Organizational Perspective*. Reading, MA: Addison Wesley, 1978.

Lucas, Henry C. "An Empirical Study of a Framework for Information Systems." *Decision Sciences*, vol. 5, January 1974, pp. 102-114.

Mintzberg, Henry. *The Nature of Managerial Work*. New York: Harper & Row, 1973.

Orr, Richard H., Pings, Vern M., Olson, Edwin and Pizer, Irwin. "Development of Methodological Tools for Planning and Managing Library Services. Parts I, II, III." *Bulletin of the Medical Library Association*, vol. 56, July 1968, pp. 235-267; and October 1968, pp. 380-403.

Schmidt, C. James. "Resource Allocation in University Libraries in the 1970's and Beyond." *Library Trends*, vol. 23, April 1975, pp. 643-648.

Simon, Herbert A. *The New Science of Management Decision*. New York: Harper & Row, 1960.

Simon, Herbert A. *The Shape of Automation for Men and Management*. New York: Harper & Row, 1965.

Returning to the Unified Theory of Budgeting: An Umbrella Concept for Public Libraries

Harold R. Jenkins

Do we need to find new approaches to traditional budgeting in order to adapt to changes in technology? Is it necessary to swing over to ZBB or PBB to make our library programs responsive to the altering of social relationships? In responding to the needs of our library patrons, do we find that we are tied down by out-moded accounting procedures? Are we beginning to think of passing the cost of interlibrary loan transactions to our users because we are handicapped by a bookkeeper's mentality, a mentality that does not allow us to think creatively about alternative options? Should our decisions to charge for interlibrary loans or to charge for indepth reference requests be seen as a cop-out, as tunnel vision, as bowing to traditional budgeting?

Herbert White has highlighted these and other concerns in his January 1982 article in *American Libraries*.[1] In that article, entitled: "Who Pays for Peripheral Services, and What Are They Anyway?", Dr. White has drawn a picture of librarians basing their understanding about "crucial library services . . . on the reality of the existing accounting structure rather than on library goals and objectives." He has pointed out that many librarians have labeled online bibliographic services as being peripheral to the library's essential needs "because they are considered expensive—which, translated, means their costs were not anticipated." From this assessment Dr. White concluded that when the need is evident, "librarians lack the flexibility to transfer dollars from the labor budget to the database vendor." Dr. White suggested a solution to the problem—the concept of program budgeting, which, he noted, few librarians follow and "even fewer administrative superiors expect if of us."[2]

I can agree with Dr. White that a sense of inflexibility may exist among librarians. All librarians can add but, apparently, some cannot subtract or substitute. The fault, however, is not with existing bookkeeping-accounting-budgeting procedures—traditional or otherwise. The fault, as

---

Harold R. Jenkins is Director, Kansas City, (Mo.) Public Library, 311 E. 12th Street, Kansas City, Missouri 64106. He is the author of *Management of a Public Library*, Greenwich, Conn: JAI Press, Inc., 1980.

Dr. White has indicated, rests with the attitude some library directors may have toward their work as managers of libraries as well as with their understanding of how to work effectively with budgetary strategies and budgetary techniques. If first they develop an attitude of wanting to determine what services and products need to be offered, they will then want to find the resources to provide new services or to improve old services by learning how to make more effective use of the total concept of budgeting.

Accordingly, all library directors will want to understand that "budgeting is an active, ongoing process of watching over the total life of the library . . . "; that "budgeting is much involved with the identification and solving of problems"; that "budgeting is the management of the decision-making process that begins with the recognition and identification of a problem and continues with a consideration of alternative solutions leading to one specific best solution to the problem."[3]

Since the Italians invented double entry bookkeeping in the 1200s, the end result of all budgeting procedures—an accounting for line items representing income balanced against an accounting for line items representing expenditures—has been somewhat the same. Getting to those line items, however, can be significantly different. Where for centuries budgeting largely followed an intuitive process, budgeting the complexity of our organizational structures today calls for a higher level of intellectual competence. Managers who budget their library operations in the future will want to see the large picture as well as its related parts within the framework of a rapidly changing technology and an altering social structure. They will want to understand that we face a long term period of unremitting inflation coupled with recurring periods when the economy will be moderately to seriously depressed. Within the context of this situation managers will want to see Proposition 13 attitudes as being healthy, encouraging and supportive of management efforts that clearly show all current expenditures as an allocation of money to buy some future value rather than as an end in themselves. In other words, Proposition 13 attitudes should be seen as a call for improved productivity rather than as a threat for further increases in tax levies.[4] Keeping these points in mind, managers in the future will want to begin to fine-tune their budgeting techniques so that they will be better able to recognize, inventory and meet the changing needs of their special clienteles.

For all public libraries, no matter what the size, the concept of budgeting is the same. In the words of James O. McKinsey, "the budget idea is very simple. It is just ordinary common sense applied to the management of a business . . . . You study what you have done, you think about what you are going to do, you formulate plans as a basis of this study and then finally you set up a proper organization to carry out these plans and see that this organization functions."[5] It was McKinsey who, as long ago as 1922, first presented the process of budgeting control "as an integrating device for gaining a broad understanding of the problems of administration."[6]

The focus of this article is directed to the concept of budgeting as the umbrella term "that covers planning, controlling, organizing and detailing each projected step of a contemplated action leading to a specific objective. Obviously budgeting should not be seen as an unwelcomed constraint but rather as a welcomed opportunity to see one's way into the future."[7]

It is this expression of an optimistic attitude that all public library managers might well affect as they look to the future. Assuming that the proper managerial attitude is one of the first essentials in launching or improving a budgeting program, we can identify this underlying "proper" attitude as one of wanting to win what is best for the library, of wanting to overcome all obstacles, of wanting to provide a quality level of library service no matter what the circumstances. Supported by a winning attitude, library directors who face fiscal restraints will want to understand that their role is one of taking their libraries into the future rather than one of merely surviving. They will want to understand that the total responsibility for getting the job done is one that belongs to the library director. It is a sensible assumption of responsibility because it places the library director in the position of saying to himself: "I am responsible. If anything goes wrong, I must take appropriate action to straighten out the situation." He continues, saying: "It doesn't really matter how impossible one or more board members may appear to be or how unsupportive the community during a levy referendum, I am responsible." This "taking the blame" is a good attitude that, combined with the winning attitude, will encourage the library director to stay on top of every facet of his library operation. Supported by this taking the blame attitude, even though others will probably not hold him to it, the library director will continue to take appropriate action to keep all of his programs on an even keel. Citing the alternative response of laying the blame upon the shoulders of others should prove the point. When we point to others as being the fault or reason why we have not succeeded, we stop taking effective steps to correct a bad situation. In a budgeting situation, when we blame others—even when such blame is appropriate, we remove the solution to our problem from our sphere of influence. We cannot control others. We control only ourselves. When we fail to do that effectively, we control nothing.

U.S. Brigadier General James L. Dozier exemplified this taking the blame attitude during a nationally televised interview following his dramatic release from his Italian Red Brigade captivity in early February 1982. He said "I am to blame. I was warned a number of times that my life was threatened. I did not take proper precautions." This was a candid appraisal that was both accurately and appropriately stated. Everyone knows that General Dozier's acceptance of blame did not hold the Red Brigade blameless for his kidnapping. It reminded us, however, that when we shift the blame away from ourselves, we deny ourselves an opportunity to play an active role in solving our problems.

The example of General Dozier's acceptance of blame can be applied to management situations. Managers who seek scapegoats when a levy fails to pass, when patrons steal books, when management becomes involved in public controversy, will fail in their efforts to resolve their difficulties. As we work through the budgeting process, as I have defined budgeting, we will fail to make effective decisions if we do not accept full responsibility for all happenings in our library situations.

There are further postures that should accompany the winning attitude as the library director approaches each decision-making opportunity. Briefly, these postures relate to the need to maintain a high level of credibility at all levels—with the board or other superior authorities, with subordinate supervisors and supporting staff as well as with the clientele served by the library. While all postures represent subjects that are treated indepth elsewhere, all are considerations that should be thought of as part and parcel of the mainframe of the budgeting process. In that sense each top management figure should work out a body of principles or guidelines to serve as a guideboard against which all decisions are measured before final action is taken. This is done to ensure top management that all decision-making opportunities are working in harmony to support a commonly held objective that in turn moves the library toward its ultimate goal of achieving a quality level of service at the lowest dollar cost.

In this discussion I am enlarging on the eighteen principles of budgeting that I identified in my book *Management of a Public Library*.[8] The suggestion is being made that the truly successful manager should have at the tips of his fingers a large body of basic principles or guidelines that will serve to modify his behavior whenever a decision is being made. While it is not my intention to provide a full inventory, there will be value in highlighting the concept I have in mind by listing a few of the guidelines that govern my own decision-making situations. They are as follows:

1. Managers should identify with the concept that the chief executive is *lent* his authority. That is the key word in the board-chief executive relationship. The chief executive has authority to act as long as he remembers that the real and final authority continues to rest with the board.
2. The operation of the library should be viewed in much the same terms as the operation of a business.

3. Every action by management should support the four principles relating to effective communication through the management hierarchy:
   a. "Each supervisor should accept and discharge the responsibility for communicating management policies, procedures and attitudes to all subordinate employees."
   b. "Each supervisor should accept and discharge the responsibility for communicating through channels to top management the concerns of subordinate staff."
   c. "Each supervisor should accept and discharge the responsibility for making changes *within the framework of the management hierarchy.*"
   d. "Each supervisor should accept and discharge the responsibility for instructing and supervising subordinates in the proper methods and procedures relating to their specific assignments and to ensure that they follow instructions."[9]
4. Management should learn to listen as well as to speak and to act effectively after the facts have been presented. It is this learning to listen to those about us, within and without the management framework, that is beginning to make a significant difference in how we manage our public libraries.
5. All labor within the library should be thought of as a resource to be developed and not as a commodity to be used.
6. Management should endorse the concept of equal pay for equal work.
7. There should be a sense of harmony in all decision-making situations. Employees should understand how everything works together for a common purpose.
8. Management should break free from traditional thinking and learn to think creatively about the solution to problems.
9. Rapport with the news media should be established and maintained at all times.
10. All planning should be done outside the framework of available funding; the implementation of plans must be within the framework of available funds.
11. Need to develop a high level of integrity. This need is particularly important to the members of the board who have lent their authority to the library directors. They cannot watch over every decision that is made. Therefore, they need to have a large measure of confidence in the integrity of the library director and an equal measure of trust that he/she will always act in the best interest of the library.
12. Need to play the library game in a straightforward manner. It doesn't pay to put something over on the community, staff or

board. All elements must have confidence that the top administrator has the best interest of the community in mind as decisions are made.

Zero Base Budgeting (ZBB) and Planning, Programming, Budgeting (PPB) represent the major concepts that have been featured as exemplary patterns of budgeting, each designed to cure economic ills wherever they exist. Each of these saw the real light of day as an individual budgeting concept following the close of World War II. Faced with the need to replace guns with cars, houses, roads and all the other accouterments of our peaceful, civilized life, for purposes of simplification there was a tendency to program the growing complexities of industrial budgets. As we have learned over the years, programming has meant separating all the parts in order that newly appointed practitioners could better understand the relationship of the parts to each other and to the whole. While this has been a concept relating to teaching and is called "programmed learning," without the name it has become a subtle process applied to budgetary situations called PPB, ZBB, PER, CPA, etc.

PPB (Planning, Progamming, Budgeting) is a formal systems approach to achieving an ultimate objective. This means that beside weighing the relative value of one way over another to achieve a nearby objective, in PPB terms we now begin to think how a nearby objective contributes to the process of achieving our ultimate objective. With PPB we are searching for alternate ways of doing things, or in demanding that the item we are paying for buys some future value.

ZBB (Zero-base Budgeting), is a term made popular by Peter Phyrr in 1970. "The label implies *tabula rasa* budgeting—an approach which would wipe the slate clean at the beginning of each fiscal year by assuming that an agency has no base from the previous year upon which to predicate its budget requests for the forthcoming year. According to such an interpretation each agency would build its budget requests from the bottom up without referring to the past as either a guide for, or a constraint upon the future."[10]

Both are interesting ideas. And necessary, too, if we are to understand the complexity of our federal bureaucracy or the complexities of our large corporate structures. All are great to read about if we have our feet on the ground and understand that if we allow ourselves to think PPB or ZBB and all the other acronyms without relating each of these to the total concept of budgeting, we could waste time and money while we allow our libraries to become enmeshed in formal budgeting structures. These individual aspects of budgeting have been pitted against the so-called traditional line item budget and the related concept of incremental increases on an annual basis.

Following World War II, particularly during the affluent 60s when the beginning inflationary spiral was almost an enjoyable, heady experience, directors of large corporations and government agencies felt that they recognized the need to break free from the limiting restrictions called incrementalism. For years a respected caveat of all conservative budgeting officers was the need to control funds by limiting growth to a marginal annual increase. Suddenly, following 1945, pressures came from every possible direction to expand services beyond the incremental level permitted by the so-called traditional budgeting concept. The ebullient feeling of a better life for everyone permeated our social structure to the very core. We were on a high, wrapped in a euphoric cloak of greater sales, larger profits for our businesses and more generous federal funding for all types of social service agencies including libraries. The initiative had changed almost over night from one of programs seeking money, to money seeking programs.

Then, just as suddenly on June 6, 1978, the bubble burst. California's Proposition 13 has represented the revolt of all the nation's taxpayers against waste and inefficiency in the management of public services, including public libraries. Since that time the economy has declined and managers tend to see a bleak financial future for their public libraries. The present reality of the situation has been capped by President Reagan's promise to move a large number of federally funded projects to local state control. The open hand held out to Washington will be withdrawn, empty.

If public library service is to survive, we will have to begin to manage, to subtract, to substitute, to think creatively about better ways of doing whatever we are doing today. This means we must learn how to budget more effectively for survival and then for the future lying just beyond our immediate grasp, but still one that can be reached.

"For purposes of accountability and control, the simpler the budget the better."[11] The introduction of innovative management tools to which we apply labels such as ZBB, MBO, PPB, PERT, CPA, tends to complicate and distort the budgeting process. "Budgeting is supposed to contribute to continuity (for planning), to change (for policy evaluation), to flexibility (for the economy), and to provide rigidity (for limiting spending)."[12]

Through the application of creative management concepts and techniques, all designed to support the traditional line item budget, today's manager can expect to take his library into the future. In guiding the library's ship through the stormy financial seas he may have to furl his sails. But if he is an effective captain he will not loose his ship, no matter what the circumstances. Nor will he have to be replaced as a result of controversy.

I have called my concept the "Unified Theory of Budgeting" or "UTB." It is a somewhat pretentious heading for an old fashioned concept, but it serves the purpose of dramatizing the need, as I see it, to return to the traditional concept of budgetary control, a concept which has always provided the best means to coordinate activities of the various departments of our public libraries and to provide at the same time a sound basis for executive control. A director needs to have at his fingertips a budgeting technique that allows his management to do whatever needs to be done for the least cost or to get the most out of a given level of expenditure in order to achieve a desired result, such as improving the quality of library service. In these modern times the need to increase or decrease spending for short run situations is important.

As I pointed out in the early part of this paper, the Unified Theory Of Budgeting begins with a statement clearly defining our reason for being in the public library business along with the assumption of a winning attitude on the part of top management. It is from this stance that effective management will develop on overall strategy and a variety of supporting tactical maneuvers, all designed to carry the library into the future. At every decision-making turn effective top management will want to keep the concept of the purpose of the library in mind. For instance, if maintaining an effective level of library materials represents the hub of the wheel, the library's reason for being in business, its reason for spending the tax payer's dollars, top management will use every appropriate maneuver in its inventory to keep the library's purchasing power for books at an acceptable percentage of the total budget expenditures. On the other hand, if top management has multiple goals and no single overiding perception as to why the library is in business, the final outcome of decision-making among competing objectives could be to produce confusion, divided loyalties and, subsequently, possible failure.

After agreement has been won about the exact wording of its statement defining the library's ultimate goal, top management should begin to plan its broad budgeting strategies. In his book entitled *The Politics of the Budgeting Process,* Aaron Wildavsky has shared his insight and understanding of budgetary strategies as they are practiced throughout our federal bureaucracy. Dr. Wildavsky has defined budgetary strategies as: "Actions by governmental agencies intended to maintain or increase the amount of money available to them."[13] He noted further that "Strategic moves take place in a rapidly changing environment in which no one is quite certain how things will turn out and new goals constantly emerge in response to experience. In this context of uncertainty, choice among existing strategies must be based on intuition and hunch, on an educated guess, as well as firm knowledge."[14]

In a manner of speaking, success in budgeting a public library is based on understanding two fundamental management responsibilities:

1. Knowing well and intimately the full scope of the library's pro-

gramming and staffing as well as the inter-relationship and cost of all operating units.
2. Knowing well and intimately and being sensitive to the political ramifications of all decision-making opportunities.

The first of these closely related aspects of management, both of which relate to budgeting, should be highlighted through the preparation of financial reports, particularly the Summary of Expenditures.[15] It is this latter report that should be designed to show the relationship of the costs for all operating units—branches, departments, etc.—to the line items contained in the annual report.

While accounting is not the total thrust of budgeting procedures, it is obvious that accounting plays a significant role in the budgeting process. The analysis of problems leads through planning to solutions and finally to the best solution. Working plans are then reduced to the common denominator of dollars and cents recorded as line items in the summary statement of the budget. Reduction of all planning to dollars and cents provides the primary base for management control, a control that will enable management to study the relationship between one function and a competing function or activity in the total library program. From this comparison decisions are made. Later they may be overturned and new decisions made.

It is the accounting role that produces the line item budget that management uses to control its operation during each current year. It is accounting that also produces the annual Summary of Expenditures referred to above that in turn allows management to surface and compare the line item cost for each of the library's operating units after the books have been closed at the end of the year.

An alert management will also prepare additional supporting financial and statistical reports, all designed to provide an up to the minute picture of any and all aspects of the library's operation.

The second aspect of management, that of being sensitive to the political ramifications of all decision-making opportunities, brings to the fore the need to be aware that this part of the budgeting process takes considerable skill and finesse based on the director's intuitive understanding of the propriety of making or not making a recommendation, of making or not making a public statement.

Some directors have developed management skills with one aspect or the other but not always with both. When the going is rough they may lose their jobs. Those directors who remain on the job for a considerable length of time have learned to cope. They have learned to handle the ever changing situations involving new board members, staff problems, overly zealous concern for what certain citizens feel the library's mission should be, etc. By hunch, by intuition, by an educated guess, by a sixth sense as well as by inside information, alert management rolls with the punches. It hangs in there and gets its library into the future through the use of budgetary strategies along with a certain knowledge as to how all departments and branches of the library system relate one to the other.

We library directors can have the best managed libraries providing the most effective level of service throughout the community—and still lose a levy referendum. It is not enough for management to know that a particular library is well managed, that it spends its funds wisely, that it gives its citizens the best possible run for each dollar spent. It is necessary that the citizens also know these facts and that they know, for example, what will happen if a new levy referendum fails to win voter approval. Even then the levy might fail. We cannot allow our more perfect understanding as managers to blind us as to the need to keep our supporting citizens informed well enough to pass a new tax. We need to dip into our inventory of budgetary strategies and to come up with a winning combination. That might have been relatively easy to do during the affluent sixties. Today, in our Proposition 13 times, putting together the proper combination of budgetary strategies may well nigh be equal to pulling Excalibur from its stone. Every library needs its Merlin.

One thing is certain—every situation is different. While we can take a particular library and document how the director handles one situation after another and wins or lose a point, no exact pattern can be developed and offered as an example for other directors to follow. I can suggest that the reader of this article look over the Summary of Expenditures that we have created in Kansas City. It is applicable to other libraries. However, this is not the case with budgeting strategies. There are an infinite variety of strategies. For instance, everything can appear to be in the same relationship and then a new director comes on the job. Suddenly, nothing is the same. Old stalemates may be broken, animosity felt by one or more board members toward the old director may disappear, the structure of the library may begin to change, etc.

Perhaps there may be some value in highlighting some of the changing factors that an alert director should be concerned about, factors that will influence his budgetary strategies.

1. A change in the composition of the board through an introduction of new members; election of new officers of the board; presence of a continuing sense of opposition to one or more pet projects proposed by the library director.
2. A critical change in the management hierarchy could in turn introduce subtle but critical changes throughout the library.
3. Expected state or federal aid payments could be sharply reduced without warning.

4. The library community could be sharply divided on key issues facing the administration of the library.
5. A citizen group could request the removal of one or more book titles.
6. The library's levy referendum might fail to win voter approval.

Using budgetary strategies is an art form. It is one that requires finesse and an intuitive understanding of what to say, what to do and where to turn at every decision-making opportunity. Success calls for the proper mix of people, ideas, money and attitudes. That is the budgetary process. It is in the successful handling of these decision-making situations that we find the fun of managing a public library.

REFERENCES

1. White, H. "Who Pays for Peripheral Services, and What are They Anyway?", *American Libraries,* 13, no. 1 (January, 1982): 40.
2. Ibid. p. 40.
3. Jenkins, H. R., *Management of a Public Library.* Foundations in Library and Information Science, v. 8, (Greenwich, Conn: JAI Press, Inc., 1980) p. 136.
4. Mushkin, S. J., ed. *Proposition 13 and its Consequences for Public Management,* (Washington, D.C., Council for Applied Social Research, 1979).
5. McKinsey, J. O., *Budgeting Technique,* Annual Convention Series, no. 51 (New York: American Management Association, 1926), p. 75.
6. Ibid., p. 75.
7. Jenkins, H. R., *Management of a Public Library,* p. 121.
8. Ibid., pp. 124-134.
9. Ibid., p. 51.
10. Lauth, T. P., "Zero-Base Budgeting in Georgia State Government: Myth and Reality" *Public Administration Review,* September/October 1978, p. 420.
11. Wildavsky, A., "A Budget for all Seasons?" *Public Administration Review,* November/December 1978, p. 509.
12. Ibid., p. 501.
13. Wildavsky, A., *Politics of the Budgetary Process* (Boston: Little, Brown, 1964), p. 63.
14. Ibid., p. 64.
15. An example of the Annual Summary of Expenditures report prepared by the Kansas City Public Library may be had by sending a request (along with a $2.00 fee) to the Business Office, Kansas City Public Library, 311 E. 12th Street, Kansas City, Missouri, 64106.

PART II:
ISSUES IN
SPECIFIC BUDGET
CATEGORIES

Salary Planning

Paul M. Gherman

INTRODUCTION

The portion of the budget devoted to personnel of most large libraries usually exceeds fifty percent. This amount is greater than those budgets allotted for collections, binding, equipment, and current expense, yet very little attention is given the personnel budget for a number of reasons. Salaries are considered an on-going expense which is generally locked into the parent organization's salary plan and with the exception of merit increases or appointment salaries are beyond the library administration's control. Unlike books or equipment, people have strong emotional reactions to salary issues, for one's salary is at the very center of the contract between each individual and the employer. Belcher in his seminal work on Salary Administration points out that salaries rely on psychological, sociological, ethical, political and status differences as the basis of the reward system.[1] Therefore, any suggested change in the salary structure meets with rapid and strong opposition from all concerned. Needless to say, because of this reason, administrators are often timorous about broaching the salary issue.

For adequate salary planning to take place, the total personnel systems must be considered and each position must be seen as relating to the issue of compensation. The ultimate goal of salary planning should be that the work of the library is adequately and precisely defined and that the appropriate levels of staff are selected to perform this work, that compensation is equitable and just, and that the salary dollars are most effectively used in achieving the goals of the organization. Longer range salary planning must also attempt to define the changing nature of work itself within the context of automation and high technology as it will affect libraries in the future.

The various elements of a personnel system which can be utilized in salary planning are task analysis, job classification, job design, career development, and performance evaluation. The efficiency of the salary

---

Paul M. Gherman has a BA in English and History from Wayne State University and a MALS from the University of Michigan. He is currently the Assistant Director for Administrative Services at the Iowa State University Library, Ames, IA 50011. He is a member of American Library Association, Association of College and Research Libraries, The Iowa Library Association and the American Society for Personnel Administration.

© 1983 by The Haworth Press, Inc. All rights reserved.

budget will be enhanced if each of these elements is consciously linked in a systematic way, clearly defining the library's work, the performance of that work, so that employees are appropriately paid for the level of work they perform.

THE MEASUREMENT OF WORK

Before salary planning can take place, there first must be a systematic method of measuring work of an organization.[2] For greater efficiency, the work of the organization should be divided up in a rational manner, and then specific jobs need to be categorized and aligned according to their relative worth to the organization. Individuals are then compensated according to their contributions by performing jobs of lesser or greater worth to the organization, or performing jobs of lesser or greater difficulty. Central to the organized assessment of jobs is a job evaluation system. Most job evaluation systems begin with a set of factors which the organization defines as measures of value. These measures of value may differ between broad groupings of jobs. Professional level jobs may be valued by the following factors as defined by Wilkinson: 1) degree of expertise; 2) independence; 3) level of formal external contact; 4) planning and development; and 5) supervision.[3] Basic production jobs performed by support staff can, however, be evaluated on a different set of values: 1) skills and abilities; 2) responsibility; 3) effort; and 4) working conditions.[4] The parent organization usually sets or adopts those values to be applied when determining the relative worth of a task or a job. These same values are then applied to library tasks and jobs as well as all other jobs within the organization. However, at the clerical level, library work generally differs significantly from other types of work within the parent organization because of the intellectual nature of library tasks. Many classification analysts are bewildered by technical library positions and tend to downgrade tasks, perceiving them to be clerical in nature.

The adequate recognition of this kind of difference within any general job classification system is extremely important to libraries. For example, in Technical Services, the intellectual process of applying varying cataloging rules is difficult to define and evaluate on the traditional scale of values. Obviously the knowledge, skills, and ability necessary to catalog a book today are substantially different as compared to just a few years ago because of changing standards and technology. The problem develops when the library must assign a relative value to cataloging tasks as compared to supervising a reading room. The knowledge and skill level of the catalog task may be higher than the knowledge and skill needed in the reading room; however, the responsibility level in the reading room may be greater. If effective salary planning is to take place, this type of value differential must be articulated, defined, and placed within the job structure. A job structure that is out of alignment with the library's needs is likely to develop if the library allows the parent institution's value system to be applied by classification analysts who have a limited understanding of the library work context. Through a point-count system, ranking system, or factor system, the library must take an active role in placing a relative value on tasks to be performed.

JOB DESIGN

Once a relative ranking of values has been determined for specific tasks, these tasks must be formed into jobs. This formation, or arrangement of tasks into jobs, is called job design. The greater the precision in defining individual tasks and the composite tasks into jobs, the more precise the wage structure will be, and therefore compensation will more accurately parallel the organization's goals. In job design, a series of tasks is assembled so each task can be accomplished in an effective manner, while also taking into account the human factor. Jobs cannot be so routine or restrictive that boredom affects productivity, nor so varied that training becomes too extensive, so that turn-over becomes costly. Each task should be of comparable difficulty so employees are not overpaid for the lesser valued tasks in their job or underpaid for higher valued tasks. However, challenging, higher level tasks added to a lower level job can sometimes motivate an employee and lead to higher levels of productivity. By thus evaluating each task in a job description, the sum total of the tasks and their point value can then place a job within point ranges of the salary structure so individuals are paid equitably for all tasks performed.

In most libraries, few opportunities exist for job design except when new positions are being developed or major reorganizations or programs are being undertaken. Yet as libraries change, so does the work of librarians, and therefore, jobs are fluid and ever evolving. In effective salary planning, a program of constant job review must be maintained so that job descriptions remain current. Not only do jobs change because of the overall evolution of the library but also because of the individuals in them. The longer the employee stays in a particular job, the more likely the person will grow more proficient in the job, accept more responsibility, and perform more complex tasks. Thus, the overall momentum of job classification system is upward. This upward movement can be justified to some extent by the changing nature of the libraries. However, much of the movement is attributed to the individuals in specific jobs striving to fulfill themselves by performing higher level tasks. If this movement or classification ''creep'' is allowed to proceed unchecked, the increased dollar costs in wages can be significant. Good salary planning must meet this issue directly and with vigilance, and the organization's need for work to be performed at specific levels must be distinguished from the employee's desire to perform work at higher levels.

As positions become vacant, a close review of the job description should be made. Positions should be reviewed for currency, and be scrutinized to see if the level of tasks has evolved upward due to the last incumbent's abilities. Also, first line supervision usually prefers that the positions are filled at the current incumbent's proficiency level, rather than reverting to an entry level position. The decision must be made whether the perceived need of the supervisor to replace an employee at the higher level outweighs the overall cost of classification "creep."

Job descriptions of long-term employees should be reviewed on an ongoing basis. Although it is difficult to reduce the classifications of positions with individuals in them, upper limits of responsibility should be placed on positions in relation to the organization's needs and not those of the individual. To alleviate some of the pressure to increase the levels of position, a system of career ladders and a defined promotional system should be developed. As employees move through the system from job to job, a recruitment and training load is created for supervisors. However, this cost should be offset by a cost reduction in the classification "creep." Additionally, as employees move from position to position, they gain a broader perspective on the library and are therefore more valuable to the library. Because of the increasing level of intelligence and education of library employees, no career ladder or promotional system will completely eliminate the pressure of their expectations nor can any library ever satisfy all employees' ambitions. A clear statement should be made to employees so that they know the limits to which a given job may evolve and the options open to them through the promotional system. Once they meet the limits of the system, they should be encouraged to move to another organization if possible.

The situation is different in those university libraries having faculty status. Parallel and sometimes simultaneous systems or tracks are used to measure the contributions for this group. Certain librarians hold administrative positions for which they are paid an increment above their base salary; however, as a faculty member, their compensation is also based on their rank, and on their meeting specific criteria for promotion and tenure. These criteria are generally teaching (librarianship), scholarship (publication and research), and service (professional activities). These criteria or values differ significantly from those stated by Wilkinson whose values relate directly to those of the library. The criteria or values for librarians with faculty rank seem to be less directly related to the overall library goals even though they may clearly support the university's goals. This division of goals between the library and the university occurs because the library's organizational structure is vertical, whereas, that of the university is horizontal. Also, the library is basically a production unit, whereas a university is not. Universities seldom place maximum limits on faculty salaries; instead, faculty compensation is based on how well each individual faculty member meets the stated criteria. Therefore, in universities with faculty status, salary differentials of librarians can be based on individual innovation and energy and not on specific tasks performed which are valued specifically by the organization. Although an immediate library goal may be the implementation of an online catalog, librarians may be highly compensated for writing articles or attending meetings which may only be partially linked to the development of an online catalog. Many would contend that there is a direct linkage between professional and scholarly activities of librarians and the developmental needs of the organization. However, there is also a critical slippage possible in this type of compensation system in these times of tightening budgets and the impending need to accomplish organizational goals. The result may be a tightening of requirements or institutional pressure to abandon status goals.

PERFORMANCE EVALUATION

The second major method for measuring the work of employees is through performance evaluation. As a job classification system defines the work of an organization, a performance evaluation system defines and measures how well the work is to be done. Performance evaluation systems can and do take on various forms, and they are perceived by management and employees as serving various ends. At one end of the scale, a performance evaluation system is used to document performance and to substantiate the retention or dismissal of an employee. In the middle ground, the system measures the employee's contributions to the library and in turn how merit pay is awarded. At the other end of scale, the evaluation system is seen as a motivator which leads to increasingly higher levels of performance and therefore greater organizational efficiency. To be most effective, performance evaluation systems should define for the employee, in specific terms, the types of on-the-job behavior which will be rewarded by the organization. One system on which much has been written is Management by Objectives (MBO). This system suggests that each employee or groups of employees set individual performance goals which support the stated organization's goals, and they are rewarded to the degree to which they meet these goals. This system is an effective way for management to both measure and motivate performances in support of the goals of the organization. Such a system is most effective when used with upper levels of professional staff who are involved with the process of defining the organization's goals. It is also effective when the work is less defined such as in the context of faculty status.

A second system may be more effective for the staff at the clerical support level who have little influence in setting the library's goals. This second type of performance evaluation system relies on a clearly defined job description made up of discrete tasks. For each task, performance levels or expectations are developed by supervisors and the employee. They agree, for instance, that the task of filing cards requires that 100 cards are filed per hour with less than a 5% error ratio. This type of performance standard is negotiable within limits and is to be rewarded through merit pay. In this system, the usual ambiguity related to performance is eliminated by specifying the exact levels of performance. The system also eliminates the discrepancy between various supervisors' judgments who are evaluating individuals performing the same task, so that performance is reviewed equitably across the organization. A common problem of an evaluation system which measures according to the standard measures of quality, quantity, initiative, and other factors, is that these measures are applied to the whole job and not to discrete tasks within a job. Employee performance can vary from task to task, so that a secretary may be a fast and accurate typist, however her filing ability may be much less acceptable. If the supervisor averages out her performance in both tasks using the above mentioned measures, this same secretary may be given an above average rank in quality or quantity. Thus, the secretary may believe that an adequate job is being done in filing as well as in typing because the evaluation is not task specific but instead evaluates the gestalt of the job. The level of performance should increase if the evaluation system is perceived by the employees as being precise and reliable and that the economic rewards correspond to the system. Often employees feel that their evaluations are not true indicators of their performance and that the corresponding merit pay systems are unfair and do not recognize their true performance. Therefore both the performance evaluation and the merit pay systems are not motivators of higher levels of performance.

COMPARABLE WORTH

Another major issue facing salary planners in the eighties could be that of comparable worth. For some time the courts have held to the principle of "equal pay for equal work." This principle is that two individuals doing the same thing should be paid the same. Most libraries have reviewed their work force to make sure that they are in compliance with this principle. However, the comparable worth principle goes beyond the principle of equal pay in that it holds that two individuals doing dissimilar work but of comparable worth to the organization should be paid the same. In other words, even though the activities or tasks of two jobs are dissimiliar, the incumbents should be paid the same, if the tasks or job point-count are the same or are considered the same when compared to a bench-mark position or class description. This position seems clear, straightforward, and obvious. However, this issue is still more complex, because the courts are now questioning that more than one classification system is used. If an organization uses two separate classification systems or value systems, such as those described earlier by Belcher and for two apparently distinct work groups, a justification must be made of these differing systems. For if the two systems of values support distinct pay scales, a defense of the varying scales must be made. For example, if the support staff of the library are classified and paid according to one system and the librarians are paid according to another system, a justification must be made for the differing systems. Because the work of libraries flows on a continuum, it is difficult to identify a clear line where clerical work ends and professional work begins. Therefore it is even more difficult to clearly defend why two distinct value systems should be applied to library jobs. If it is necessary to classify all library jobs according to one system, significant dollars may be necessary to adjust the system and the differentiations between clerical work and professional work will need to become far more explicit.[5]

THE CHANGING NATURE OF LIBRARY WORK

The more difficult part of salary planning is the longer range necessity of planning for future personnel needs and making accurate judgements about the numbers and levels of staff to implement the varous evolving library programs. Central to this rapid change in libraries is the impact of technology which increases in speed and proportion in an arithmetic progression. A great deal has been written about technology and its impact on bibliographic organization, services, and in some ways the nature of libraries. However, little has been said about its impact on job classification and personnel costs to libraries.

A prime example in the recent past has been the shift to publishing in microform. Microforms are far less expensive to purchase and they take up far less space to house. However, the personnel costs to maintain the equipment, store and access the collection, and train the patron in their use are considerably higher than paper copy. In one academic library with a collection of just over 1 million pieces of microform, the annual personnel costs are conservatively $60,000. As this collection grows, and especially as the Superintendent of Documents shifts to increased levels of micropublishing these personnel costs will rise accordingly at a significant rate. It is doubtful that libraries actually calculated the personnel costs when the acquisition decision to shift to micropublishing was made. There is still no algorithm for personnel costs per piece of microform. However, despite the evident difficulty in developing appropriate staffing levels the above example is simplistic when compared to the complexity of the problem when the impact of computer technology is considered.

As the computer and high technology become more pervasive in libraries and the publishing world, the role of libraries will shift dramatically. The work load emphasis will shift from the acquisition and the arranging of information to the accessing of information stored and retrieved electronically. As acquisition budgets decline in the face of inflation, resource sharing via networking will supplement the actual purchase of materials. On demand publishing and new levels of cable transmission will significantly change the current nature of both technical and public services in libraries. Eventually these changes should bring about a reduction in staff and an eventual savings of personnel costs. However, during the transition stage, the time when technology is implemented will be more costly because of the redundancy caused by the necessary planning and development effort. If libraries are to survive this technological transition, they must plan and budget for adequately trained staff to accomplish the task.

An early misconception about technology was that its advent would reduce personnel costs, since the machine could perform certain tasks more efficiently and at a more consistent quality than humans. However, this reduction in personnel costs has usually occurred at the low end of the salary scale where employees perform routine and repetitive tasks that a machine can more easily perform. Allen Veaner in a recent article "Management and Technology" states that "Technology has certianly reduced many of our unit costs, but it has not reduced total costs. Indeed, total costs have gone up. There are several reasons for this. First, the personnel costs of new technology tend to be higher."[6] The cause for this rise in personnel costs is that the very nature of work changes from the routine to the conceptual, from the mundane to the creative, so therefore, the lower paid employee is replaced by the higher paid employee. Peter Drucker says it this way: "Automation certainly brings about an ever greater rigidity of labor costs. Labor is no longer direct production labor but 'indirect' and 'overhead labor.'"[7] In other words, as libraries implement high technology, direct labor such as typists who create catalog cards are no longer needed; whereas, systems analysts and greater numbers of managers are needed to develop and maintain the technology. If book acquisitions were to drop, theoretically the typists could be laid off due to reduced work load, or if fewer reference questions are being asked, the number of reference librarians could be reduced. On the other hand, technology must be maintained at the same level no matter what the acquisitions level or the use of the library. Thus planning for the personnel costs to implement the new technology is indeed a most challenging task. The advantage of turnkey systems is the reduced personnel costs, because the developmental costs for the software are distributed across the potential number of users of the system. A recent adage in the field of microcomputers is to select hardware not on the basis of its features but on the availability of software that can be used on the hardware.

The cost of automation is the cost of personnel. Precise personnel planning probably cannot be done in such an environment because the nature of work has shifted from production to creative and developmental work, and this type of activity cannot be quantified as production work. Not only does technology itself add to personnel cost, but it has also established the need and ability to network and create national bibliographic systems. Participants of these systems can no longer act or exist independently as they once did, but they must comply with national codes and standards. Change at the national level therefore means implementation at the local level, whatever the personnel costs. When AACR II was adopted, most of the major libraries in the country were faced with major efforts to evaluate its impact on the local level, plan for its implementation, and finally make the considerable changes necessary for its implementation. Although extensive consideration and evaluation were given to the impact of this change on the bibliographic system and its costs, little or no thought was given to the personnel costs related to this change.

With technology the very nature of the work becomes more difficult and job classification levels shift upwards. Because libraries have a history of procedure and practice embedded in their bibliographic systems, the transition period during which technology is adopted and refined is especially difficult. Manual systems must be maintained in parallel to the automation systems, and the retrospective conversion of the total system will be a lengthy process. In the intervening period, simple jobs become more complex because of these parallel systems.

A clerk typist once typed the catalog cards according to local procedures. With the use of OCLC the typist no longer had to type these cards. However, to produce these cards it became necessary to know the rather complex protocol and structure of the OCLC system. AACR-II was then accepted and these new rules had to be overlaid on the use of the OCLC data base. The complexity of the work has moved upwards considerably along with the pay classification. Multiply this by a host of different library jobs and add to it impending changes in technology, networks, bibliographic standards and utilities, and the magnitude of the planning problem becomes apparent.

Hours must be spent by management planning, developing, and implementing the systems made possible by technology. Hours and days are now spent at the local, state, regional and national level in developing the concept and system of what libraries will become. Because of the complexity and pervasiveness of technology, more and more librarians are being involved at the operational level. Truly Peter Drucker's comments about "indirect" cost assuming a major proportion in an automated environment are well founded. Allen Veaner realized this complexity in the automated environment when he said, "The work must be broken down into comprehensible units of practical size. This requires development of comparatively independent, isolated service modules—which when finally interconnected may result in a complex system which is less flexible than the manual counterpart. In such a complex structure it may take months or even years to implement a seemingly modest design change."[8] Up until now we have had little or no experience in planning for the personnel costs related to the indirect costs of development or change of this nature, and only with further experience will we be able to develop the appropriate algorithm. Yet, without this algorithm many libraries may not bring their development efforts to reality because of the lack of adequate planning for personnel. For years conversion to automation was out of the reach of librarians because of the cost of the hardware. Today hardware costs are declining at an amazing rate, while at the same time personnel costs are rising. Melvin Hurni, in an article a number of years ago, speaking of business, "we have entered an era in which competition for concepts about the basic nature and structure of business is coming to be as real as competition in the market and in the research laboratory."[9]

In libraries today we also have entered this same competitive situation. Private industry has realized that information through the use of automation and communications, has a vast potential for profit. The recent court decision allowing AT & T with its vast pool of capital, research facilities, and communication networks to enter the information market place could potentially increase the speed and extent to which this change will take place. Recently the *Harvard Business Review* announced it will be published in electronic format with the text available via computers.[10] Should the many scholarly journals follow and AT & T step in as the transfer agent, libraries may soon find themselves in a far different role. Thus libraries are not just faced with the automation of our manual systems, but we must define our role and market share in this competitive environment. Indeed the issue may be survival itself.

In conclusion, the issues facing administrators doing salary planning are destined to be complex and as challenging as the library environment itself. Salary planning must no longer be ad hoc or an after thought, but it must be actively practiced in a systematic way if libraries are to plan for the future and have the necessary personnel to accomplish the dramatic change that libraries will undergo.

REFERENCES

1. David W. Belcher, *Compensation Administration* (Englewood Cliffs: Prentice-Hall, Inc., 1974), pp. 1-10.
2. Belcher, *Compensation Administration*, p. 87.
3. John Wilkinson, Kenneth Plate and Robert Lee. "A Matrix Approach to Position Classification," *College and Research Libraries* 36 (September 1975): pp. 351-63.

4. Belcher, *Compensation Administration*, pp. 140-41.
5. Allen B. Veaner, "Continuity or Discontinuity—A Persistent Personnel Issue in Academic Librarianship," *Advances in Library Administration and Organization* 1 (1982): pp. 1-20.
6. Allen B. Veaner, "Management and Technology," *IFLA Journal* 7 (1981): p. 34.
7. Peter F. Drucker, "Integration of People and Planning," *Harvard Business Review* 33 (November/December 1955): p. 38.
8. Veaner, "Management and Technology," p. 34.
9. Melvin L. Hurni, "Decision Making in the Age of Automation," *Harvard Business Review* 33 (September/October 1955): p. 52.
10. *Information and Data Base Publishing Report* 3 (March 19, 1982): p. 1.

Interlibrary Loan and Resource Sharing: New Approaches

Noelene P. Martin

The effectiveness of a national system of interlibrary lending is directly related to the equitable distribution of costs among all the libraries involved. *National Interlibrary Loan Code,* 1980.

The changes that have occurred in interlibrary loan over the past ten years have dramatically increased its importance as a basic library activity. Before the advent of online union catalogs sponsored by nationwide bibliographic utilities the difficulties in discovering the existence and availability of wanted materials ensured that interlibrary loan would be used only in cases of dire necessity. The procedures involved and the time taken resulted in an expensive "special" service. That it was one which frequently rescued a researcher from failure was often overlooked in assessing its importance.

Relegation to peripheral status of interlibrary loan ensured that the initial attention of automation would be directed to cataloging and circulation, both large scale operations and visibly labor-intensive. The librarians concerned with patron needs, however, quickly realized that they had at hand a new tool of unparalleled potential. Suddenly the platitudes that have for so long been accepted as defining resource sharing were overtaken by a new reality and it is no accident that the first new subsystems developed by OCLC and RLG were for interlibrary loan.

CHANGE OF PACE: THE EXTENDED BIBLIOGRAPHIC NETWORK

Although extensive review of the changes wrought by the technology is not appropriate here,[1] a brief description will help set the scene for further consideration of its financial implications.

The most important change has been the great expansion of access to bibliographic information. Libraries which could not afford more than the

---

Noelene P. Martin is Chief, Interlibrary Loan Department at the Pennsylvania State University. She has been Chair of the Interlibrary Loan Committee of the Reference and Adult Services Division of A.L.A., Chair of the Clearing House for Interlibrary Loan Committee on the Pittsburgh Regional Library Center, and a member of the OCLC Interlibrary Loan Advisory Committee.

© 1983 by The Haworth Press, Inc. All rights reserved.

most basic tools can now have online access to indexes and union catalogs that were once available only in the largest libraries. The new information covers not only books, but areas not previously covered, such as technical reports, dissertations and music.[2] As was made clear in the surveys conducted for the U.S. Copyright Office "both computer searching as well as ILL can be characterized as activities which can enhance or supplement local library collections and services irrespective of library size."[3]

The second change relates directly to the technology involved—a dramatic increase in the speed of communication. Sending an interlibrary loan request via terminal is much faster than using the U.S. mails. This enhancement has the unfortunate side-effect of greatly increasing user expectations—which cannot be fully satisfied until better means of document transmission are available at a reasonable price. Nevertheless a first, important step has been taken in reducing one of interlibrary loan's principal drawbacks, the time taken—though it should be noted that the acquisition of materials is even more time consuming. User reactions to time in both these cases are an interesting commentary on their attitudes to library services. Users will wait for something to be acquired but are very impatient when it is a case of borrowing.

The third change is the currency of the new information. While even the union catalogs of the utilities contain information on recent publications, the most dramatic improvement has been in the indexing of periodicals. Online information is available long before its printed counterpart and, though the titles covered may be limited, for such fields as science and technology the greater up-to-dateness cannot be questioned. Moreover the flexibility of computer access allows cross-searching on a scale impossible for any manual system.

Finally, all libraries, large and small, who participate in the networks now have access to information about locations, even for materials published as recently as a month or so ago.

THE IMPLICATIONS OF THE NEW TECHNOLOGY

Librarians have found multiple uses for this enhanced bibliographic universe. It makes verification quicker and simpler, whether the purpose is ordering, cataloging, borrowing, simply identifying an item, or determining its existence. It also enables reference librarians to extend the range of their services. Because databases frequently contain anlaytics and similar entries, often not in the library's own catalog, their use can provide more information about the library's own collections. For collection development purposes the record of locations may play a significant role (The Research Libraries Group made this a focal point of its program), but for interlibrary loan the vast extension of information on titles and their locations has offered a new way of operating.

If an item is not owned by a library, the fact that the material actually exists, i.e., that it has been bibliographically identified, suggests that it should be available, without delay, through interlibrary loan, no matter whether it was published a century, ten years or ten days ago. Since it is frequently easier and faster to borrow than to purchase, there is the temptation to rely on borrowing and, in fact, interlibrary loan is cheaper.[4] Here the codes remind librarians that such transactions should be confined to the state or regional level,[5] and that all libraries have a duty to collect the materials needed regularly by their own constituents.

The entry of the computer into the interlibrary loan scene has begun a revolution whose effects have not yet been felt or understood. The extension of bibliographic control is a clear enough example of improved working conditions leading to higher productivity and better service. Its effects on user expectations have not yet been incorporated into conventional wisdom. If an item can be tracked down, it can be provided for the user. The implications of this for collection management have not been realized. Although attention has been drawn to the use of interlibrary loan records for collection development purposes,[6] no systematic attempt has been made to incorporate such information into collecting policies.[7] One of the problems has been the temporary nature of many interlibrary loan demands. Once the specific research project has been completed, those materials may never be needed again. It is clear also that borrowing emphases shift over time, but all libraries should be aware of what is being requested by their users. One of the side-effects of the new Copyright Law has been renewed attention to multiple requests from one journal, leading to the need to decide on buying rather than borrowing, though budget restrictions have made systematic response difficult for many libraries.

There are those whose faith in the computer is such that they run the danger of excessive reliance on computer systems. "It's not in the computer" has become equivalent to "It does not exist." The ease with which a machine can be used and the deceptive completeness of its message combine to lull users into a sense of dependence. Despite the enormous increase in information available there are still more materials not in the databases than are. Hence there is still a need for professional discrimination in the use of the computer in relation to other mechanisms.

The difference between finding out about something and actually obtaining it is also significant. Many look forward to the day when the full text of documents will be readily available online. Already LEXIS and NEXIS provide such services—at a high cost, which may sometimes be worth paying for important information. But, on a more reasonable level, interlibrary loan makes it possible to provide cheaply, on demand, copies from originals stored in other libraries. The service is not instantaneous and it is only the exigencies of actual delivery methods that cause the delay.

INTERLIBRARY LOAN COSTS

Changes of such magnitude have financial implications. Whereas previously an Interlibrary Loan operation probably had only a typewriter or two and a telephone and, possibly, a TWX machine, it has now to be tied in to one or more networks with terminals and printers, probably has several banks of shelves where materials are set aside for special delivery systems, and almost certainly has more people doing more work. The cost of this change, while not great in itself, represents a considerable growth in a department which was usually the smallest in the library or a dependency of Circulation. The literature warns against expecting good interlibrary loan service from a shared terminal, but in most libraries ILL is still forced to cope by using, say, an hour a week at the Catalog terminal. While this may be adequate for a very small operation it places very serious limitations on the use of a tool whose key characteristic is instant access. Whatever the arrangement, the fact is that ILL must now be tied into any network—at a cost—and, if there is any local delivery network, it provides the reason and the need for participation. Increases in workload have led to increases in staffing, even if only at a student helper level or by transfer. It is likely that, for the first time, most library managers have become aware of interlibrary lending as a cost—which worries them because they are still unaware of the benefits. If these costs were compared to the cost of acquiring and cataloging an item, the perception would change. Interlibrary loan while expensive when compared with circulation on a transaction basis is much less expensive than acquiring an item. The range of interlibrary loan costs reported in the literature is $5-10 per transaction. The costs of acquiring and cataloging an item range from $30-$100, to which has to be added the $1 a year needed to retain the item. It is not clear whether all these figures include the same element or what allowance has been made for various overhead costs. Nevertheless it is clear that the cost of purchasing something is by several magnitudes greater than the cost of borrowing something.

In an analysis of "peripheral" operations Herbert White makes the telling observation that "we focus on them [i.e., expenditures] when we should be talking about services, access and objectives to be met for our clientele."[8] The new costs are substitutional costs and may well have greater benefits than added expenditures on other activities. This is particularly true for smaller libraries which are unlikely, in any circumstances, to be able to extend their materials budget, yet these are the libraries which have felt unable to increase their expenditures on interlibrary loan (read resource sharing).

Here is an elegant opportunity for deciding the return on expenditure. As noted earlier, participation in a utility not only improved cataloging but brought to the participating library *for the same expenditure* access to the equivalent of an enormous range of bibliographic publications. The books were, in effect, obtained free. In like manner, the use of online data bases is not only a service, but a subscription to indexes and abstracts, which could not otherwise be provided. This dual perspective on payments for contracted services has generally been overlooked by libraries, and ignored in budgeting.

THE EFFECTS OF NETWORKING

The rapid growth of networks has inevitably led to complications. There is some evidence that we are in a shaking down period. Some existing services have been phased out, e.g., Pacific Northwest Bibliographic Center (PNBC) and the interlibrary loan service of the Bibliographical Center for Research (BCR).[9] Yet others which came into existence to meet new needs, have in turn been replaced by newer services.[10] Dorothy Russell, in describing the work of PALINET, refers to one of the results of new networks thus: "The effect of using different bibliographic utilities is that libraries speak different languages."[11] This increases the problems of interlibrary loan and separates libraries. From a slightly different perspective Charles Hildreth in a study of online catalogs stresses the need for the development of a more effective user interface.[12] Since interlibrary loan transactions are essentially with an online catalog these comments are pertinent and address a persistent problem in library automation. Nevertheless it is clear that computerized networks are here to stay and it should be the goal of libraries and utilities alike to exploit the benefits, overcome the problems and develop new services. In fact, when used in an integrated ILL system the utilities offer possible enhancements such as better record-keeping, statistics and billings, particularly at local and regional levels.

The concern expressed by many major libraries that they would be overwhelmed by requests does not appear to have been borne out, though it is true that patterns have changed substantially. In part this is due to the fact that many more libraries are participating in ILL, in part to the fact noted by Daniel Gore that "students and faculty are already reading about as much as they can,"[13] but mostly to the fact that the numbers of active participants have increased greatly, thus spreading the load.

The effects of automation have therefore been both positive and negative and these advantages and disadvantages are listed in Figure 1. This mix of good and bad is to be expected in any new development and the listing is meant to spur attempts to remedy the defects.

Figure 1

The Contribution of Automation to Interlibrary Lending

Advantages	Disadvantages
1. Bibliographic Information	
Increase in scope, particularly in information about locations.	Limitation to participating libraries, resulting in parallel universes
Increase in speed in making the information available	Emphasis on current rather than retrospective information
2. Communication	
Increase in speed in message sending	Increase in volume of messages
Establishment and enforcement of protocol	Conflict with existing protocols
Enlargement of the network	Overlap with existing networks
Easier multiple communication	Tying of communication possibilities to the network system
3. Availability of Materials	
Potential of transfer by electronic means	Increased expectations beyond current means of satisfaction
Aid in collection development Tools for resource sharing	Neglect of local collection building
4. Costs	
Establishment of standard costs for requests	Defensive charges levied by net lending libraries
Potentially-better records	Introduction of further cost elements
Potentially - new methods of handling cost transfers between libraries	Development of multiple networks with different procedures
	Increase in operational costs from increased volume of work

INTERLIBRARY LOAN IN RESOURCE DEVELOPMENT

In this new bibliographic world the role of interlibrary loan in the library's resource development program needs reassessment. Organizationally and functionally, Interlibrary Loan is usually conceived as a kind of circulation department yet, since its role, for members of the institution, is the procurement of materials not in the library its true ally is acquisitions. Unless this relationship is recognized Interlibrary Loan is unlikely to be able to take its proper place in the library's resource program. Given the problems that libraries are having in maintaining their acquisition rates,[14] it is surprising that more attention has not been given to substitutes for ownership, particularly for increasingly expensive, specialized serials. Despite various studies comparing the costs of owning and of borrowing[15] there is little evidence of any systematic attempt to include interlibrary loan in statements on collection policy. The same, incidentally, is true of the purchasing of materials through commercial database services. Both these examples show the firmly entrenched nature of organizational concepts which make difficult the coordination of separate activities when one has traditionally been a technical and the other a public service.

True, much research and study has to preceed any more general application of the idea. To date most research has gone into the costs of interlibrary loan itself.[16] These are useful as benchmarks by which to measure one's own costs but they are only one side of the necessary equation. To a certain extent the groundwork has been laid by the many studies that have been carried out in connection with the new Copyright Law but these have tended to concentrate on the effects on publishers and authors, only tangentially on the effects on acquisition.

There have, however, been several useful articles on the more general principles of resource sharing[17] which have begun to enunciate new groundrules for cooperation. The impact of the new electronic networks has undoubtedly contributed to this development. Even so simple a thing as the development of a Union List of Serials or a Union Catalog on Microfiche can change radically the ways in which libraries operate.[18] Such possibilities became realistic expectations only with the widespread application of computer technology. Their development and the effects have been rapid and have not yet been fully assessed. What have not yet been evident are any large-scale reconsiderations of collection development goals nor re-examinations of the role of interlibrary loan together with a recognition of the needed support.

FINANCIAL IMPLICATIONS

Such reconsideration must, however, now be central to any library's financial planning. If proper use is to be made of increased access to external resources libraries must be prepared to transfer from funds intended to support the acquisition of materials sufficient money to support increased interlibrary loan and database searching. As Gore suggested, in the article cited above, owning something that is not used is expensive and so is the continued borrowing of something that is not owned. Between these extremes, however, it is possible to find many areas where occasional access is best served by borrowing or by purchase of the specific article required. Such responses eliminate altogether the extremely expensive matter of processing, which is often neglected in comparisons between owning and borrowing.[19] If we also take into account the cost of storage and the construction of new facilities the case for resource-sharing becomes overwhelming. The exercise of imagination and initiative is sorely required. "The savings in costs of acquisitions must be balanced against the costs of borrowing, and cost accounting methods in these procedures are not always the most precise. It is essential to have a well-delineated and functioning interlibrary loan network by means of which resources can be shared to back it up. And this is one place where libraries have more or less fallen down nationally . . . [OCLC has helped to facilitate ILL] but it has done very little to help manage the fiscal problems underlying the whole system."[20]

The present chaos which exists in terms of charges between libraries and charges to users indicates that libraries have not yet given the necessary consideration to a growing segment of library activity, so that no coherent philosophy of access to information has emerged in spite of the endless articles on "free or fee."[21] In the same way as circulation has been clericalized and downgraded, interlibrary loan has been regarded as peripheral and in both cases the sudden advent of automation has caught libraries unprepared for change. The question is seldom asked whether $30,000 from an acquisitions budget might not return the library substantially greater benefits if used for increased interlibrary loan staff and the payment of borrowing costs for photocopy instead of the subscriptions to the journals themselves. Yet this is precisely the kind of question that must be asked with increasing urgency, if libraries are to survive in an age of budget-cutting.

Although not necessarily directly related to interlibrary loan, the growth of electronic publishing has clear service and cost implications for all information services. Some of these new ventures are substitutes for traditional publishing, others, notably the program outlined by COMTEX,[22] envisage a new kind of publishing designed to shorten the time between the development of an idea and its dissemination. Again while it is a matter of examining substitutional costs, it is also a question of re-examining the functional organization of the library and the allocation of costs among these functions. This re-emphasizes the importance both of the program redefinition advocated by Javarkovsky and of the new modes of decision-making recommended by Bommer elsewhere in this issue. Both approaches must take into account the effects of the new fluidity of information and the electronic infrastructure that carries it. The boundaries between Reference, Circulation, Interlibrary loan and Acquisitions are artificial and may well be impediments to the proper exploitation of these new resources. A library program for resource acquisition must now include parts of all these traditional functions and must consequently result in a new budgetary model.

The development of models for this kind of budgeting will be slow and tedious, but it is urgently needed. Studies similar to those undertaken of the relationship between circulation and collection building must be undertaken. The ultimate goal is to determine levels at which cooperative acquisition and resource sharing can be effective in meeting a library's source goals. These must be balanced by a clear view of the likely effects on publishing, if libraries were to reduce drastically their total number of subscriptions.[23] New consideration has to be given to temporary acquisition techniques, usually characterized as online ordering. Clearly the importance will vary with the library and the needs of its users, but all libraries are faced with the impermanent needs represented by short-term projects and the passing needs of users.

Libraries have eagerly exploited the extension of their bibliographic access as it applies to cataloging, but have not yet seen how the same access can revolutionize reference and interlibrary loan, and help bring about the resource sharing that has been preached for years. The needs and the problems were thoroughly aired at the 1973 and 1976 Conferences on Resource Sharing in Libraries, held at the University of Pittsburgh. The proceedings of both conferences, published by Marcel Dekker, repay close study by any librarian with a commitment to resource sharing. Again the requirement is to look at the existing facts from a new perspective, that of service to the user, rather than that of traditional collection building.

The new techniques emphasize personal access to information and, if that access is hidden away in technical service areas, users will tend to go outside the library and develop their own contacts. To combat this libraries need to examine the cost-benefits of information access from another standpoint—that of the user. Consumer-oriented studies can determine when direct access to materials is required—the core collection—and when the access needed is to one specific item best provided on demand. Of course, that also implies that the material is held elsewhere and requires a library-to-library commitment to work together to develop commercial resources. The political problems of such a changed approach cannot be minimized. For so many years the size of a library's own collection has been its claim to fame and a shift to emphasizing its services would be seen as revolutionary. In fact, the revolution has already happened, outside libraries, and the requirement is to reconnect the library to the new information systems.

REFERENCES

1. Noelene P. Martin and M. Sandra Wood, "Interlibrary Loan in the Computer Age: The Impact of Online Systems on Document Delivery." *The Reference Librarian* (in press)
2. Sharon Cline Farmer, "RLIN as a Reference tool," *Online* 6 (5): 17, Sept. 1982.

3. *Libraries, Publishers and Photocopying: Final Report of Surveys Conducted for the United States Copyright Office.* Washington, D.C., 1982. pp. 2-37, 2-38.

4. Daniel Gore, "Nothing Succeeds Like Excess," *Library Journal* 107 (14): p. 1378.

5. Ann T. Dodson et al., "Electronic Interlibrary Loan in the OCLC Library: A Study of its Effectiveness," *Special Libraries* 73 (1): 12-20 (Jan. 1982). The point is made that regional service was faster and most cost-beneficial.

6. P. Thorpe. "Interlibrary Loans analysis for journals acquisitions," *Aslib. Proc.* 31: 312-9 Jl'79

7. This does not imply that individual librarians have not been aware of the potential. In personal discussion Hendrik Edelman stated that he required all who requested large numbers of interlibrary loans to be referred to him for discussion, to see whether the libraries at Cornell should be buying more in that area.

8. Herbert White, "Who pays for 'peripheral' Services and What Are They Anyway?" *American Libraries* 13 (1): 40, 44. Jan. 1982.

9. "BCR Ending Interloan Service and Closing Union Catalog," *Library Journal* 107 (14): p. 1367, Aug. 1982.

10. "MIDLNET throws in the towel," *Library Journal* 107 (14): pp. 1366-67, Aug. 1982.

11. Dorothy Russell, "Interlibrary Loan in Network Environment: The Good and the Bad News," *Special Libraries* 73 (1): 21-26, Jan. 1982.

12. Charles R. Hildreth, *On Line Public Access Catalogs: The User Interface.* Dublin, OH: OCLC Inc., 1982. (Especially Chapter 5.)

13. Daniel Gore. Op. cit. p. 1376.

14. For example, "Research Libraries' Collections Hit Hard by Inflation," *Chronicle of Higher Education,* January 22, 1980, plff, but the literature is full of studies of the effects of inflation.

15. King Research, Inc. has conducted several research projects over the last ten years.

16. For example: J. E. Herstand, "Interlibrary Loan Cost Study and Comparison," *RQ* 20: 249-56, Spr 1981, and S. A. Roberts, "Internal Costs of Interlibrary Lending in British University Libraries," *Interlending Review* 9:101-3, July 1981.

17. Notably Richard De Gennaro, "Copyright, Resource Sharing, and Hard Times: A review from the Field," *American Libraries* 8:403-405, Sept. 1977, and "Resource Sharing in a Network Environment," *Library Journal* 105: 353-355, Feb. 1, 1970 and the symposium edited by S. Y. Crawford and B. E. Markuson, "Perspectives on: Library Networks and Resource Sharing," *American Society for Information Science. Journal* 31: 403-444, Nov. 1980.

18. E. A. Breedlove, "Impact of COM Statewide Union Catalogs on Resource Sharing," *Catholic Library World* 52: 272-275, Feb. 1981.

19. Murray S. Martin, "Buying, Borrowing and Bibliographer: Some Observations on Collection Development Flexibility," *Library Acquisitions: Practice and Theory* 3: 117, 1979.

20. David A. Kronick, "Goodbye to Farewells: Resource Sharing and Cost Sharing," *Journal of Academic Librarianship* 8 (3): 134-135, July 1982.

21. Yale M. Braunstein, "Cost and Benefits of Library Information: The User Point of View," *Library Trends* 28 (1): 79-87, Summer 1979. There are several pertinent references in this article to the hidden cost of services and who benefits from them as well as useful observations on organizational costs.

22. *Chronicle of Higher Education,* Oct. 6, 1982, pp. 25-26.

23. In fact, the effects are likely to be less drastic than feared by publishers. In just the same way as some studies have exaggerated the role of interlibrary loan and photocopy, the spectre of cancelled subscriptions has been overblown. Even studies by industry sources suggest that in the area of highly specialized publishing the relationship is with the major research libraries and is relatively stable. (Quirk, Dantia *The Shrinking Library.* White Plains. Knowledge Industry Publications, 1982. p. 87). Most smaller libraries never would have subscribed to such journals and do not have the financial resources to do so. More equitable access to needed articles, either by borrowing or by electronic means, is what is required.

Financial Planning for Collection Management

Frederick C. Lynden

PLANNING FOR A LIBRARY MATERIALS BUDGET

There are many facets to the planning and preparation of a library materials budget request, and estimation of the costs of library materials is only one aspect of the process which a library must consider. Indeed an accurate appraisal of a library's materials budgeting needs should be a continuous process which does not end when the budget is finally declared. There are numerous factors which must be taken into account, including cost research, economic conditions, political factors, environmental and historical variables, and administrative considerations. Each of these factors will be examined in detail in the paper which follows. The planning process ideally must involve not only most segments of the library staff, but also many parties outside the library. Although this paper will study the university research library environment, many steps of the process have application in other types of libraries. Certainly, the research which must occur before, during, and after the actual budget has been settled is common to any library situation and the other aspects of planning would have equal importance in all types of libraries.

COST RESEARCH

Three basic sources exist for gathering information about the prices of library materials: professional sources, book and periodical vendors, and local studies. First, there are the professional sources of information. The American Library Association sponsors indexes for hardcover books, paperback books, periodicals, serial services, library produced microfilm, media, and newspapers. These price indexes are published regularly in the *Bowker Annual of Library and Book Trade Information* with an interpretive essay by the current Chair of the Library Materials Price Index Committee (LMPIC), Resources Section, Resources and Technical Serv-

---

Frederick C. Lynden is Associate University Librarian, Technical Services, Brown University Library, Providence, RI 02912.

© 1983 by The Haworth Press, Inc. All rights reserved.

ices Division, American Library Association.[1] For those who desire early information, much of the data for these indexes appears earlier in various forms. For example, the twelve month hardcover and paperback price information appears early in the year, February or March, in *Publishers Weekly*, in an article edited by Chandler Grannis.[2] In the fall, the eighteenth month figures are printed in the September or October issue of *Publishers Weekly*. Other advance data appear in the *RTSD Newsletter*. The *RTSD Newsletter* is now reporting foreign price information (Great Britain and Germany) earlier than it appears in the *Bowker Annual*, and is covering the annual preliminary information on American periodicals (usually available in January at the Midwinter meeting of LMPIC).[3] The Library Materials Price Index Committee will accept inquiries from anyone regarding price information.

Other sources of professional information are: *Library Literature*, library annual reports, and colleagues. *Library Literature* cites many articles on material prices. These articles are customarily entered under the heading ''Books—Prices''; ''Periodicals—Prices''; and ''Serials Publications—Prices.'' Unfortunately, the index is not current enough to provide citations for the most immediate data, but background articles on the costs of materials at libraries can be very helpful for comparative purposes. To keep up-to-date on changes, the academic budget planner should regularly read *Publishers Weekly, Library Issues: Briefings for Faculty and Administrators, Library Journal,* the *Chronicle of Higher Education* (not indexed in *Library Literature*), the *ARL Newsletter,* and the *RTSD Newsletter*. Library annual reports also provide useful information on how libraries are coping with rising costs. The University of Pennsylvania annual report has been especially valuable over the past four or five years for its analysis of the costs of library materials. These reports often give one a view of the approach a particular library has taken in dealing with a college or university administration. Finally, many libraries have formed informal groups for the exchange of information on budget requests. One such group is the ''Gnomes'' a group of seven private university libraries. It is frequently useful to cite the cost rise at other similar institutions when justifying a request.

A second principal source of information is the book or periodical vendor. F. W. Faxon, Inc. has been producing periodical price study since 1974. Until the past year this study has appeared in the October *Library Journal*. In 1981, the *Serials Librarian* published a continuation of the Faxon study.[4] Of particular value is the chart showing the average price paid by institutions from July 1975-June 1981. This chart, produced annually, shows the changes in average prices paid for periodicals by colleges and universities as well as other types of libraries. Academic book suppliers have been producing annual price data for some time now. The Blackwell North American (BNA) company has been providing price data to the university and college library community since 1975/76. The B.N.A. price studies present average prices by subject classification for university press and approval plan books. Similar information is now available from Baker and Taylor, Ballen, and Coutts, all wholesalers who provide approval plan service to academic institutions. The Library Materials Price Index Committee is currently trying to synthesize such data into a "research library price index," but until they do, it is possible to obtain information from these vendors on the costs of "research" materials. Some foreign vendors (e.g., B. H. Blackwell and Otto Harrassowitz) have also offered price information for their blanket order plans. Both of these companies can offer customers computerized printouts with price data. A consulting firm, Research Associates of Washington, publishes the annual *Higher Education Price Index,* an academic price index which has a book and periodical component. Until last year, it was produced at the Office of Education and the Department of Education. Compiled by D. Kent Halstead, it includes index figures for American books, American periodicals and foreign books.

Foreign book price data have always been difficult to obtain, and as a result many libraries compile their own studies based upon information from foreign blanket order or approval plans. These local studies, including total number of titles, total cost, and average cost per title compared over several years, can demonstrate the high costs of foreign materials. There are also a number of foreign sources which can be used, and a 1977 article on the costs of overseas publications cites many of the library associations, national libraries, government organizations, and bodies which publish European book price statistics.[5] One organization in particular should be mentioned since it produces an academic book price index. The work done by the Library Management Research Unit (LMRU) of Loughborough University in England is of special interest to academic librarians. For over five years, the LMRU has produced a British academic book price index based on books deposited at the Cambridge University Library under copyright provision and selected for the library as suitable for academic programs. The index, originated by James L. Schofield, is now produced by Alan Cooper of LMRU.[6] Another source of foreign price information covering the entire world is the annual Library of Congress survey on foreign book prices which is customarily published in *LC Acquisition Trends.*[7] The LC survey is the basis for foreign book price data in the *Higher Education Price Index.*

A third principal source of information is the local cost study. Many libraries are now compiling their own cost studies since it is the mix of materials which are purchased locally which determines local increases. There has been controversy in the past about the value of using local studies instead of national data. The consistent position of the compilers of national data has been that the national indexes were never meant to replace local studies but rather to serve as a national standard to be used for comparative purposes. Local studies have become more sophisticated as more libraries have automated acquisition systems which can provide accounting. One study done at Harvard on the costs of periodicals at Harvard showed close correlation with the national indexes.[8] The Association of Research libraries has published a SPEC (Systems and Procedures Exchange Center) Kit on *Library Materials Cost Studies,* including samples of cost studies from libraries surveyed. The survey showed that the majority of libraries relied on published sources and indexes, but indicated that a number of efforts were underway "to create more meaningful indexes and studies" since administrators do not find the national indexes especially relevant to their local purchases.[9]

A number of institutions have prepared local cost studies over several years. Prominent among them are the universities of Chicago, Stanford, and Purdue. (Examples of these local studies were included in the ARL SPEC Kits on *Library Materials Cost Studies* and *Cost Studies* and *Fiscal Planning in Research Libraries.*) Another source of institutional data for ARL libraries is the Collection Analysis Project (CAP). For example, the MIT Libraries did a general analysis of library materials costs as a part of the final CAP report and recommendations. Included in the analysis was a historical overview of the buying power of the budget showing the loss of buying power in current dollars compared to constant dollars.[10] The CAP program includes a module on reviewing and analyzing materials fund allocation practices, and most published CAP reports will have a segment analyzing the materials budget allocation process. Local reports can be helpful in three ways. First, they can lead to new sources of published information. Second, they can be used for comparative purposes. Finally, they can aid in demonstrating possible approaches to take in soliciting funds.

Informed budgetary planning requires background reading, and the body of literature on library budgeting is expanding. Three recent examples are: Sul H. Lee's *Library Budgeting: Critical Challenges for the Future,*[11] Murray Martin's *Budgetary Control in Academic Libraries,*[12] and Michael E. D. Koenig's *Budgeting Techniques for Libraries and Information Centers.*[13] These three works provide excellent background on important considerations in library budgeting, and offer advice relating to the purchase of library materials. Other recent literature on collection development discusses aspects of budgeting for materials. Hugh F. Cline and Lorraine Sinnott's book *Building Library Collections*[14] looks at fund allocation and expenditures for collections, and the two volume work, *Collection Development in Libraries,*[15] by Robert D. Stueart and George B. Miller, Jr., also includes a paper on budgeting for collections. Another recent article focuses on materials budgeting in private university libraries, citing over fifty articles or books which deal with some aspects of budgeting for library publications.[16] Two works by non-librarians approach library budgeting from a macroviewpoint. *Economics of Academic Libraries*[17] by William J. Baumol and Matityahu Marcus and *Scholarly Communication: the Report of the National Enquiry*[18] both consider the broader issues of concern to library budget planners, e.g., library growth rates: cost trends for journals and books; technological innovation, and national systems for storage, bibliography, and preservation.

ECONOMIC CONDITIONS

In planning for a budget request, it is extremely useful to be aware of economic conditions both nationally and locally. One must be familiar with the rationale for price indexes. An excellent explanation is given in the government document, *Higher Education Prices and Price Indexes,* by D. Kent Halstead, Washington, 1975.[19] The planner must know how the prices of materials have changed relative to the Consumer Price Index, a national measure of the prices of a fixed group of consumer goods since most budget requests show how library materials costs have fared in relation to the general cost of living. It is also important to be able to measure the increase in foreign costs. The International Monetary Fund journal, *International Financial Statistics,* includes data on the exchange rates for foreign currency which can be used for conversion purposes in budgeting. Some budget requests include provision for loss in purchasing power due to devaluation of the dollar.

It is also important to observe the financial trends in one's own institution of higher education. Many universities publish budget figures in their official newsletter. Two examples are Brown and Stanford. In other schools the information is not so readily available. Librarians planning the materials budget should obtain a copy of the university or college annual financial report. Frequently this report will include an expenditure and income line for the libraries, and this information can be used in showing the ratio of expenditure for the library in comparison to university educational and general expenditures. Even when there is no separate line for the library, it is important for the budget planner to be familiar with an institutional financial annual report.

It is also helpful to be able to cite economic conditions in the publishing industry and in libraries in general. A most valuable compilation of data regarding the publishing industry is contained in the annual *Book Industry Trends* published by the Book Industry Study Group.[20] Other sources of data are the (publishing industry) reports in *Publishers Weekly* on areas as printing, paper manufacture, and marketing of books. One must keep alert to ad hoc groups which are studying the economics of libraries. In October 1981, the Association of Research Libraries sponsored a meeting to examine issues in the *Economics and Financial Management of Research Libraries,* and the participants agreed as a next step to study the "feasibility of creating a broad financial planning model for research libraries . . . "[21]

A preliminary report from that conference indicates universities have used a variety of budgeting systems "such as zero base budgeting, the Planning Program Budgeting System (PPBS), and computerized models such as Stanford University's Trade-Offs System (TRADES)—each with its benefits and weaknesses."[22] Both the Stanford and the Brown University financial planning models contain a materials budgeting component.

ENVIRONMENTAL AND HISTORICAL VARIABLES

Certainly the size of the institution and scope of its programs will affect any planning for book and serial funds. Many institutions have special forms for making materials budget requests which take into account: the users—faculty, graduate students, and undergraduates; special faculty research interests; new programs; research grants available; and local resource sharing arrangements. Examples of these forms are available from the ARL Collection Analysis Project at the University of California at Berkeley and the Massachusetts Institute of Technology. The number of graduate and undergraduate programs as well as enrollment will have an influence on the collecting needs of the library. The location of the institution as well as its historical associations with other institutions will govern its ability to obtain needed materials quickly from other libraries. Many institutions now have excellent reciprocal agreements with other schools which would directly affect the budget proposal. For example, The University of North Carolina and Duke have special country assignments for Latin American collection development. These types of special program commitments may change the size of the materials budget.

The historical strength of local collections, as well as special funds, will also determine the content of a library's material budget. There may be a special request in a budget for the support of a nationally renowned collection which can no longer be supported by endowment funds. Collection evaluations may show slippage in certain subject areas where retrospective support will be needed. Special program support which has dwindled may need to be restored. Grant funds which have been the mainstay of a collection may no longer be available, and the collections will languish if there is no adequate support. In 1977, for example, a Princeton University Committee on Library Acquisitions and Losses argued that there had been a dramatic decline in purchasing power at Princeton resulting in a shift in the budget away from the Humanities and Social Sciences to the Sciences. In turn, this shift had severely damaged the strength of the collections in the Humanities and Social Sciences. The outcome of this report was the approval of a level of funding which restored the purchasing power of five years before, and the extension of a special allocation for lost books for six more years.

Student enrollment and the degree programs contribute directly to the amount of usage a collection receives. One element in planning a budgetary presentation is information on enrollment and degree programs. For example, large graduate enrollments in History may be a factor in causing the library to argue for a special supplement to the history allocation. Likewise if there is a new program on Japanese Studies or on Egyptology, the library must gather information on the cost of materials which would support it. The planner should make an effort to learn about these curriculum changes and program enrollment trends as early as possible. At Brown University Library, the Faculty Library Committee, on the advice of the University Librarian, recommended that all proposals for new degree programs include a library impact statement. This suggestion has become part of procedure, and the Library is always asked to assess the collection impact of any new program. This requirement has resulted in proper financial support for collections in new areas where the university has begun programs.

POLITICAL FACTORS

Selling a library materials budget is clearly a political process, especially in these days of double digit inflation. Even though general inflation rates have fallen, the special problems of publishing, which have always caused library materials prices to be above the general consumer price levels, remain; e.g., low demand, high production costs and expensive materials. Therefore, much planning and preparation has a political aspect. One crucial element in selling a materials budget to the university is effective communication. In addition to articles in the campus daily, alumni magazine, and employee bulletins, there must be regular and frequent communication about the cost of library materials with the faculty, provost, and university budget officer.

To avoid surprises, the Library should plan to keep university administrators and appropriate faculty up-to-date on the local library financial situation. One method of apprising them of the broader situation is to send them *Library Issues,* a newsletter which contains information on library materials costs, preservation, automation, etc. Of course, frequent consultation is desirable. A second critical factor in convincing a university administration of library needs is past and current credibility. If the library staff has kept the proper records and the library administration can present factual evidence of its needs without overstating its case, then an atmosphere of trust will grow. It is important for a library to be able to show its accomplishments and its failures, and to give credit where it is due. A third political factor is the tone, the clarity, and brevity of the request. If the library is always making demands without clearly stating the rationale for its requests, the chances of failure will be increased. It is also important to make any budget proposal succinct with accompanying documentation only where such evidence is required.

A fourth consideration is an alliance with the faculty in presenting a budget. There must be careful planning to insure that, when necessary, the Faculty Library Committee has an opportunity to see the Library's budget proposal before its submission to the administration. Some libraries also have very effectively marshalled the support of faculty through the compilation of desiderata lists which have gone unfilled due to lack of budgetary support. The University of North Carolina has received special funds over the past few years for the purpose of filling lacunae on a large desiderata list. Lastly, there must be an awareness of other campus priorities on the part of the library administration. There is no substitute for keeping informed about campus policies and politics. If locally it is the year for financial aid to be the prime issue, the library may wish to keep a low profile and understate its needs. This tactic may insure the passage of its "modest" request.

Another important political consideration is competition with other institutions of similar size and stature. With the current competition for students it is not simply a strategem of librarians to show how library resources contribute to the strength of the institution. In other words, it is not a purely "political" tactic to promote the Library as a drawing card for one institution over another. Taken in this context, comparative statistics can show relative strength of a library's resources and services. ARL and ACRL statistics can be used to show the changes in position of the local library in comparison to other libraries in institutions of the same caliber and size.

ADMINISTRATIVE CONSIDERATIONS

There are a number of administrative considerations when planning a library materials budget request; the local cycle for requests; staff participation; presentation of the request; endowment and gift funds; serial vs. books funds; pressure from other parts of the library budget; and fund raising and allocations. In preparing for the budget request, it is useful to make a calendar of deadlines as well as a list of *dramatis personae.* The calendar and list can be used in assigning staff who are most concerned with the preparation of the request. Although there is ordinarily a small group concerned with such a request: the Collection Development Officer, the Business Manager, the Technical Services Chief, and the Acquisitions Librarian, many libraries have found it helpful to involve larger numbers of staff, particularly selectors. The principals involved may also wish to contact the American Library Association, vendors, publishers, or other institutions to obtain the most up-to-date information. Staff in the Technical Services area can be queried regarding local costs. The selectors should be queried regarding local costs. The selectors should contribute information about their needs. At the University of Chicago, there is a formal questionnaire for selectors which asks questions for each subject specialty about the rate of scholarly publication; the cost of books and journals; changes in enrollment, faculty, curriculum or research activities; anticipated large expenditures; and the addition or elimination of any subject areas or special formats of materials. At Stanford, the business officer meets with every department to discuss the library budget to insure that every department contributes to its construction.

There are a number of possible approaches for presenting a materials budget request. All require the library to recommend a rate of increase based upon local figures, comparative library computations, national cost experience, or combinations of the three. Most libraries apply the increase against their budget base from the previous year. This calculation would be a maintenance increase. The number of variations from this basic format are many, but the common ones build improvements into this base. Many libraries add additional funds for new programs while others add funds for retrospective needs. Some libraries request a special fund to prevent erosion of the budget through devaluation of the dollar against foreign currencies. Other libraries calculate the number of academic publications which the library must acquire in order to remain current. Still other libraries show justification for restoring budgets where they have been cut, or provide an itemized list of expensive purchases which could not be purchased due to prior levels of funding. Some libraries explain what will happen to collections at various levels of increase, providing the administration with a program choice. Finally, many ask for one time, capital increases to fill in lacunae identified through a collection evaluation. All of these budgeting approaches demand extensive preparation.

All materials budgeting proposals must account for certain common variables: the cost of books and journals; the extent of endowment and gift support; and the pressures from other segments of the library budget. The phenomenon of double digit journal inflation is too well known to repeat here, but it does affect the preparation of the budget. The planner must include differential rates of increase for books and journals. Some vendors will now provide a library with serial expenditure data which can be very helpful in the budgetary process by showing increases resulting from a specific selection of titles. Because the cost rise of serials has accelerated at a much faster rate than that for books, many libraries have placed restrictions on the level of serial expenditures, and this limitation affects planning for the materials budget. Many libraries have a special fund for new serials in order to take some of the pressures off of the general materials budget. A second factor affecting the budget proposal is the extent of gift and endowment support. Librarians must make university administrators very aware of the restricted nature of endowments and gifts so they will not overestimate the value of such funds to the library. Likewise when such funds are raised, there should be advance agreement that the funds will be used to enhance the materials budget rather than replace general funds. A third factor affecting budget planning is competition with other library needs. Many libraries require larger and larger sums to support personnel and automation. It is always better to make a separate case for acquisitions despite these competing demands. The faculty will generally support a special case made for funds for collection development.

The allocation process usually occurs after a decision on the budget has been made. However, librarians who are planning ahead can use allocations in a political fashion. If faculty members are unhappy with their allocation, the library should make them participants in the next year's budget process by asking them to define their needs more precisely. Unfilled requests, missed retrospective purchases, the lack of major microform sets, or the need for specialized materials can be used in next year's round to buttress an argument for increased support of the materials budget. The allocation process can also demonstrate real needs. Those allocations which are either overspent or have the largest number of requests outstanding against them, may be the areas where the Library will have the best case for negotiating increases in the future. Where departmental allocations are used and these allocations are consistently underfunded, university departments have been known to raise special funds to augment the library allocation on a one time basis for retrospective purchases.

One other administrative consideration is fund raising for library materials expenditures. As more and more demands are placed upon the beleaguered university general budget, it is wise for the Library to consider its own fund raising program. In universities and colleges where there is a development office, conflicting responsibilities will need to be resolved, but it is helpful to dedicate some staff time to such activity, be it through a specific person or through a Friends' program. By employing a full-time staff member in the Library, the University of Chicago was able to increase significantly its gift, endowment, and grant funding for collection development. The University of Chicago also has a Friends' group which actively solicits funds for materials. The Newsletter of the Friends' group occasionally has advertisements of expensive items which the library has not been able to obtain. The Stanford University Libraries publish a glossy version of the library annual report for the purpose of recognizing donors' generosity as well as keeping them informed on library activities.

CONCLUSION

This paper has not prescribed a particular scenario for the planning of a materials budget proposal, but rather included a description of the various factors of which any solid proposal must take account. Every institution has its own idiosyncracies and, as a consequence, it would not be helpful to propose a single course of action. Nevertheless, most materials budget requests must contain at least the following components: a statement on the current status of publishing costs and prices; a description of the Library's collection needs as well as its standing among comparable institutions; a proposed percentage rate of increase, based on some comparative data; data establishing the Library's need for such a rate of increase, based on documented local and comparative figures; and information about collection goals and priorities. As noted above, there may be special requests with special justifications, such as a contingency fund for large purchases or a reserve fund for devaluation costs.

Research has indicated that university administrators are best persuaded by: 1) the inflationary increase required to maintain current purchasing levels; 2) arguments showing the value of maintaining and increasing library collections which support research and teaching; 3) faculty support of the library's proposed budget; 4) the honesty and integrity of the library administration; and 5) ranking among comparable libraries. Librarians must be aware of the administrative, political, economic, environmental, and educational factors described in this paper to prepare the type of case which will convince university administrators. Despite the strongest case it is sometimes not possible to increase the budget to the degree required. Then, it is incumbent upon the librarian to continue the analysis to show how the past budget was inadequate, and what effects inadequate funding has upon library collections. At the same time, librarians should be considering how they can lessen the impact of shrinking funds on collections through more precise definition of collecting goals and objectives, expanded resource sharing of lesser used materials, increased utilization of available collections, and decreasing other library costs.

REFERENCES

1. Williams, Sally F., "Prices of U.S. & Foreign Published Materials," in *Bowker Annual of Library & Book Trade Information,* 1981, New York, R. R. Bowker, 1981, p. 340-353.
2. Grannis, Chandler, "1981 Title Output & Average Prices: Preliminary Figures," *Publishers Weekly* 221:42-46 (March 12, 1982).

3. Leonhardt, Thomas W., "Library Materials Price Index: British Book Prices," *RTSD Newsletter,* 6:40-44 (July-August 1981); Brown, Norman & Phillips, Jane, "Library Materials Price Index: Preliminary Survey of 1982 Subscription Prices of U.S. Periodicals, *RTSD Newsletter,* 7:15-16 (March/April 1982).

4. Lowell, Gerald R., "Periodical Prices, 1979-1981 Update", *The Serials Librarian,* 5:91-99 (Spring 1981).

5. Lynden, Frederick C., "The Cost of Overseas Materials." *LEADS* 16:6-7 (December 1977).

6. Cooper, Alan *Average Prices of British Academic Books, 1978.* Loughborough, England: Library Management Research Unit, Loughborough University, 1979.

7. "LC Book Receipts, 1979 and 1980," *LC Acquisitions Trends,* 9:35-40 (February 1981).

8. Williams, Sally F., "Construction & Application of a Periodical Price Index," *Collection Management* 2:329-44 (Winter 1979).

9. Association of Research Libraries. Office of Management Studies. Systems and Procedures Exchange Center. *Library Materials Cost Studies,* SPEC Kit No. 60, January 1980, Washington, D.C., Association of Research Libraries, 1980.

10. Association of Research Libraries. Office of Management Studies, Systems and Procedures Exchange Center. *Cost Studies and Fiscal Planning in Research Libraries,* SPEC Kit, No. 52, March 1979. Washington, D.C.: Association of Research Libraries, 1979.

11. Lee, Sul H. *Library Budgeting: Critical Challenges for the Future.* Ann Arbor, MI: Pierian Press, 1977.

12. Martin Murray. *Budgetary Control in Academic Libraries.* Greenwich, CT: JAI Press, 1978.

13. Koenig, Michael E. D. *Budgeting Techniques for Libraries & Information Centers.* New York, NY: Special Libraries Association, 1980.

14. Cline, Hugh F. & Sinnott, Lorraine. *Building Library Collections: Policies & Practices in Academic Libraries.* Lexington, MA: Lexington Books, 1981.

15. Stueart, Robert D. & Miller, George B., Jr. *Collection Development in Libraries: A Treatise.* Greenwich, CT: JAI Press, 1980.

16. Lynden, Frederick C. "Library Materials Budgeting in the Private University Library: Austerity & Action," *Advances in Librarianship,* v. 10. New York, NY: Academic Press, 1980.

17. Baumol, William J. and Marcus, Matityahu. *Economics of Academic Libraries.* Washington: American Council on Education, 1973.

18. *Scholarly Communication: the Report of the National Enquiry.* Baltimore: Johns Hopkins University Press, 1979.

19. Halstead, D. Kent, *Higher Education Prices & Price Indexes.* Washington, U.S. Government Printing Office, 1975.

20. Neumann, Peter H., *Book Industry Study Trends,* 1981, N.Y. Book Industry Study Group, Inc., 1982.

21. "Economics of Research Libraries Meeting," *ARL Newsletter* 109:8 (December 4, 1981).

22. Association of Research Libraries, Office of Management Studies. *The Economics and Financial Management of Research Libraries: a Resource Notebook.* October 14, 1981, Washington, D.C., 1981. [Available to participants only—a report has now been published.]

Budgeting for and Controlling the Cost of *Other* in Library Expenditures: The Distant Relative in the Budgetary Process

Sherman Hayes

INTRODUCTION

Libraries have, for various reasons, divided their line-item budgets into categories of salaries, materials, and *other*. In the next few pages it is my intent to take you through an odyssey of explanation as to why this is so, definitions within this technique, suggestions for improvements, and speculations on future techniques related to the *other* category.

My initial approach, like all librarians, was to do a literature search. What little discussion there is in the literature, is found in more general articles on budgeting or a specific cost analysis article on a subcategory of *other* such as computer costs.

The following analysis is, therefore, a personal one, based more on my experience and my perception of the subject, than on a learned summary of literature in the field. It is hoped my observations will strike a useful chord in the reader's situation. At least, if my analysis seems completely off base, evaluate your own budgetary techniques to make sure they are working!

DEFINITIONS

Budgeting as a term is used in so many ways that before one can analyze or even define *other* within a budget, one needs to decide what is meant by *budget*. Budgeting most often refers to the techniques which allocate resources to meet the library's goals and objectives. Many people confuse financing and revenue generation with budgeting. You must plan how revenues (resources) are raised. Then, after you know that exact or

---

Sherman Hayes is Assistant to the Director at the University of North Dakota, Grand Forks, ND 58202. He has been an active member of the Budget, Accounting and Costs Committee of the Library Administration and Management Association, for which he edited Primer of *Business Terms and Phrases Related to Libraries.* (LAMA, 1978)

projected figure, you allocate the resources within a budget. Where it becomes confusing is that the budget document and plan are most often the tools prepared to justify a request for funding. *Before you have the funding you must say how you will budget it!* It is difficult, therefore, not to slip into a usage which implies that raising funds and allocating them are the same thing. I am concentrating in this paper on the allocation of resources, control and monitoring of resources, and stretching those resources most effectively within a budget.

The term *other* within a budget is definitely a concept of line item budgeting. In line item budgeting, each category is separated by the type of expenditure. All personnel costs are a line, books and periodicals are grouped together and traditionally what is left is the *other* part of the budget.

This line item technique is in contrast to program budgeting techniques, which build from the program and service division of goals versus the type of expenditure. Program budgeting is useful and growing. However, even within program budgets there usually are subcategories to assist the manager in identifying needed resources and controlling their use. If you divide your budget into service area programs (such as reference, circulation, collection development and others), you probably analyze program budgets to determine costs related to personnel, materials and *other* within them.

Much of the library literature notes efforts to break away from a line-item mentality as a budgetary technique since it does not address the programs and goals analysis needed in a modern library. However, line item budgeting is *de facto* the most prevalent method, as dictated by the organizations (e.g., State Universities) within which library budgeting occurs. Line item budgets may lend themselves to the tendency of simply adding an inflation growth factor each year or expanding the materials budget without analyzing needs, goals and objectives. Whether using line item or program budgets, one needs always to relate the budgetary process back to goals, objectives and needs to be met by resources made available to the library for budgeting.

Finally, a definition of *other*. After you allocate for personnel (salaries/fringe benefits) and materials (books/periodicals/AV/microforms) what you have left in needed support categories is *other*. Equipment is either included or excluded depending on local situations. Sometimes equipment is combined with any construction as capital improvement and therefore not part of annual operating budgets. Equipment is included as part of *other* if it is normal expansion/contraction of equipment such as regular acquisition and replacement. A major equipment purchase related to physical remodeling/expansion of building or new construction is not part of the normal annual budgeting process.

OBSERVATIONS

1. Allocation and analysis of *other* costs/budget items is necessary in both line item and program budgeting systems.
2. *Other* categories should always be evaluated within a library's goals and objectives and not just added to or subtracted from the budget as non-related to the mission of the library.

WHY OTHER?

It is logical that a triad concept for line item division of budgets has grown up in library usage. Libraries, from their inception, have been in the business of providing information and assistance for finding and using that information. This business is materials and labor intensive. There have always been the incidental items tied to acquiring materials, supporting personnel, and providing the facility needed to house the operation, thus the category *other*. The three-way division reflects the historical emphasis on physical materials and services.

Materials and people are common to almost every library, therefore the statistical comparisons and surveys for information have been most consistent in this area. The federal and state governments ask the questions farily uniformly on how much is spent on salaries and materials but have evidently found it impossible to standardize the remaining area because they ask for *other*. *Other* is difficult to subdivide because local conditions, more than standard budgeting techniques, dictate what is included in this category.

After all of the above disclaimers on how varied this category is, it is still necessary to the definition to list some typical categories. Following is a list of areas that have been included in *other*:

> utilities, office supplies, cleaning/custodial supplies, equipment, service contracts, photocopy materials, travel, conferences, research costs, consulting costs, insurance, rents, leases of building, equipment and services, computer costs, cataloging services, telephones (sometimes included in utilities), other communications systems (TWX, teletype), postage, maintenance costs of building and equipment, vehicle costs, printing and forms costs, public relations/advertising and, finally, miscellaneous.

OBSERVATIONS

3. Due to the local variety as to what is included in *other*, there is no national standardization of the category, such as in personnel and materials.
4. Since most libraries are part of a parent institution, the specific

breakdown of subcategories within *other* is generally dictated by that institution's budgeting categories and techniques, not by any strong logical division inherently developed for library usage.

THE SIZE OF OTHER

Just how much of most budgets go into this category? Using as a source *Digest of Education Statistics 1981* (National Center for Education Statistics) we find reported the percentage breakdown of expenditures as shown in Table 1.

TABLE 1. Breakdown of expenditures taken from *Digest of Education Statistics* (National Center for Education Statistics).

Category	1973-74 %	1978-79 %
Salaries and Wages	69.2	71.9
Materials	23.6	19.9
Equipment	5.6	5.1
Other operating	1.6	3.1
Number of Centers surveyed	74,625	71,037

College and University Libraries

	1974-75 %	1978-79 %
Salaries and Wages	60	60
Materials (including binding)	32	32
Other expenditures	8	8
Number of Institutions surveyed	2972	3122

Largest 50 College and University Libraries

	1978-79 %
Salaries and Wages	61
Materials (including binding)	30
Other	9

Public Libraries

	1974 %	1977 %
Salaries and Wages	58	58
Operation and Maintenance (includes wages and salaries)	10.5	12
Supplies and Materials (including binding)	18.5	16
Equipment	2	1.5
Other expenditures	11	12.5

TABLE 1. (continued)
Sample Medium Size University - Normal Budget

University of North Dakota   1978-79 %

Salaries and Wages   40
Materials   54
Equipment   0.8
Other   5.2

Sample Medium Size University - Full Cost Budget*[1]
(includes all contributed costs/expenditures from other sources)

University of North Dakota   1978-79 %

Salaries and Wages   46
Materials   40
Equipment   2
Other   12

What at first seems like a wide variety of budget/expenditure patterns among library types shows, on closer analysis, a great consistency on how money is allocated in libraries. Considering equipment within "other", you get this comparison for the categories for 1978-79.

	Public School Libraries	Public Libraries*	College and Univ. Libraries
Salaries and Wages	71.9	70	60
Materials	19.9	16	32
Other	8.2	14	8

*1977 figures used.

My analysis of contributed budget to our library indicates that we are very close to 12% in the *other* category. I would conjecture that Public School Libraries and College and University Libraries have a much higher percentage of hidden budget expenditures provided by the parent institution budget or federal government than do most public libraries. The outside limits for *other* would seem to be 5-20% of the total budget of a library.

In answer to how big is *other* we again find ourselves describing what it is not, more than what it is, because the local definition varies so greatly. *Other* is *not nearly as significant in size* as salaries and materials. The comparison of various years indicates that it has not radically changed as a share of library budgets to date.

OBSERVATIONS

5. If a library has the need to radically reduce its expenditures, then *other*, which seems to be traditionally the first place to look for savings, is not significant enough to save the main budget allocations of staff and materials. To reduce the budget greatly one has to address reducing staff and materials acquired.
6. A significant amount of *other* budget is hidden in contributed services/costs which come from separate units within the parent institution or from outside institutions such as the federal government. A full cost budget would demonstrate a more accurate analysis of the share *other* takes within resources allocation.

TECHNIQUES FOR CONTROLLING OTHER EXPENDITURES

The following section offers some comments on how to control and analyze selected *other* subcategories.

Utilities

Control of utility cost has grown as a major library budgetary issue. The library has two separate possible control mechanisms: 1) change the suppliers of and/or the type of energy used; 2) conserve energy, using physical change in facilities, change in comfort to the user and staff, change in hours to reduce use of utilities.

If a library does not apply analysis and budget control of utilities (whoever pays for it) then they or the parent institution will, in essence, allow a reallocation of budget resources by default, generally at expense to some other area of the library's program.

Telephone

Long distance calls and regular service are two separate areas to analyze. New technology in the phone systems can contribute to cost reductions as well as contribute to efficiency increases for the staff. Quantity purchase of long distance access, such as WATS lines, has been employed successfully by many libraries to reduce costs. Reasonable control mechanisms for long distance calling are common to most libraries.

However, control of long distance costs and the need to communicate by a communicating institution seem to be always in natural conflict.

Supplies

The need for controls in supplies varies with the size of the institution and the attitude of the staff. I advocate, as the most effective means of budgetary savings, using the techniques of quantity bidding and purchasing care, together with the replacement of brand names with generic products of equal quality. Elaborate systems of control, using requisitions and supply staff, need to be constantly analyzed to make sure that the controls do not cost more than the supplies being controlled. Over-control can also signal distrust of staff reasonableness and not budgetary constraints.

Travel and Conferences

Perhaps if travel and conferences were more properly placed in the larger budget, they would be part of personnel costs. This technique may be an excellent way to increase their size by combining them into the personnel budget and into the planning as staff development.[2]

Service Contracts

The continuing budgetary debate is whether one should pay for fixed service contracts or pay for each service call as needed. Each library has to analyze its ability to take risks and the repair records for a wide variety of service contracts including those related to buildings and equipment.

Some large institutions or groups of libraries have found it beneficial to transfer *other* service contract costs into new personnel who work for the institutions to perform the same functions. Some libraries do not have sufficient ongoing funds for maintenance and repair service and in essence budget these costs into new equipment at some early point in the future.

Postage/Freight

Long standing techniques still pay dividends; such as selective use of postcards, bulk mail if applicable, and other ways to reduce costs of U.S. Postal Service mailing. I am sure libraries are fully exploring non-U.S. Postal Service mail companies for select delivery such as buses, UPS, and even electronic mail.

Insurance

More than most *other* categories, insurance is not controlled by rules made by the library. The parent institution or state laws generally dictate the levels and amounts. The librarian can be most influential in making sure the coverage is logical to libraries, such as, deciding on full-cost recovery methods for collection insurance or some other plan. Just because outside experts have great influence, this does not absolve the librarian from regularly evaluating both coverage features and costs, looking toward the most optimal combination.

Vehicle Costs

A surprising number of libraries find themselves in the vehicle fleet business, whether it be vans, cars, or bookmobiles. Normal purchasing and business management techniques are best applied here; such as bulk gas/oil purchase, flat rate service contracts with a local garage if there is no staff maintenance monitoring vehicle routes to reduce mileage (if possible without service decreases), and all of the common sense vehicle maintenance techniques we use on our personal vehicles. In some select cases, one could even see an outright leasing arrangement as more economical than the library owning and servicing vehicles. For those of us who use institutional motorpools, we must always evaluate that seemingly easy method versus paying for outside rental vehicles or reimbursing staff use of personal vehicles.

Equipment

The ability of libraries to get equipment money is so varied, I am leery of repeating the obvious maxim: have a long term systematic plan of regular replacement for all equipment and follow it. Too few libraries have the resources to replace equipment this efficient way. If your budgeting pattern has been like most I've seen, then the plan is, *get equipment any time you can generate a budget for it!* Equipment can be the edge to meeting growth and user pressure without increasing staff; equipment can stretch your staff efforts. Almost all new services have some equipment costs which must be considered. Be reminded, however, that the equipment costs seldom stop with the initial purchase of equipment. An area where there is exciting potential is the area of staff support equipment. Librarians must provide equipment necessary to assist the public such as microform, audio-visual and other types. But equipment such as office equipment (automated typewriters, collators, electric staplers); custodial equipment (self-propelled vacuums, rug cleaners, trash compactors); computer equipment (OCLC, RLN, other services and local automated accounting systems); business equipment (coin changers, counters and wrappers, calculators, copy machines); communication equipment (paging systems, terminals, facsimile printers, answering machines); and many other categories can and do enhance the final service to the user by making the staff more effective and efficient. The budget rationale for this equipment should be service-oriented, just as is a new cassette player for the public. Freeing staff with machinery does provide opportunity to improve service.

Computer Service

With the growth in the use of computers, this budget category is becoming one of the most interesting and difficult to plan for. The first problem is whether any computer costs even belong in the *other* category. Accounting, acquisition and business support computer costs are probably very logically placed in *other* as support costs.

Cataloging services can be viewed as either *other* support costs or integral costs to materials. If considered as cost of materials, then direct computer costs such as line charges, service contracts, service fees could be budgeted in the materials budget. In our library, we view cataloging computer costs as incremental to the cost of materials and they are charged into our materials budget. This is more a historical choice than a specific budget decision, except that our *other* budget categories have not received the support for growth that our materials budgets have, so we find it logical to charge this major expense to materials. Another library may have just as good a reason to separate all cataloging costs into *other*.

On-line or batch searching of computer data bases for the public is an even more difficult choice to budget. Categorizing bills for telephone costs, printing and CPU time seems to be closer to *other* than materials; however, the user is receiving a direct product not much different than other information from traditional books and periodical index sources, particularly in the case of off-line printing. The product is a material, the means to the product is *other*. Computer budgeting problems, more so than any of the *other* categories, may call for the techniques of program budgeting versus line-item budgeting.

OBSERVATIONS

7. The subcategories of *other* support the contention that this category will have great *cost* increase pressures for the foreseeable future. Computerization costs, utilities, postage, vehicles costs and telephones are just a few costs which have escalated tremendously in the past few years. *Other,* just like materials and personnel, has more pressure to increase in cost than to decrease.
8. My uncertainty as to placement of items into various categories in-

dicated a two edge for *other* planning. It is very flexible in most cases, allowing creative use of the resources and budget distribution. It is also so flexible at times that the planning and monitoring functions are not working because the funds do not tie back to a goals and objective statement.
9. Just as in materials and personnel, *other* budget categories have a history of momentum to continue one year to the next as existing. Administrators must resist that momentum and analyze each category each year, or even more often, looking for savings, efficiencies and expansions which contribute to the service objectives of the library.
10. Computerization and new equipment technologies may, in the future, equal materials as a budget concern for libraries.[3] If labor as a planning component stops growing or even shrinks, then service enhancements may have to come from technology which offers new services and stretches the staff available. In fact, this future statement is probably closer to being a present statement for most libraries.
11. Even though there is great flexibility in many areas of *other* budgeting, this area has several potential legal and technical questions to be alert to, such as leasing, rents, and insurance. Do not approach them casually.

SUMMARY

The past predicts that, in the future, librarians will need to work creatively in the area of *other* budgeting techniques and costs analysis in order to maintain or even grow in their services to their users.

As long as librarians continue to relate whatever categories they use in the *other* budgetary areas back to the needed services dominated by materials and personnel planning, then *other* will not be a secondary consideration but an equal consideration in overall planning.

Other categories have some flexibilities that make them available as opportunity funds to enhance the library. They are both the underpinning of the institutional machine and the lubricant which can keep your library flowing. Their mismanagement and underutilization can slow your library down or even bring it to a grinding halt.

REFERENCES

1. Sherman Hayes, "What Does It Really Cost to Run Your Library?" *Journal of Library Administration* 1(2):1-10, Summer 1980.
2. Charles Martell and Richard M. Dougherty, "The Role of Continuing Education and Training in Human Resource Development: An Administrator's Viewpoint," *Journal of Academic Librarianship* 4(2):151-155, May 1978.

3. To a certain extent this is already evident in the published statistics of the Association of Research Libraries, where fifteen out of a hundred academic libraries reported other expenditures of over $1,000,000 in 1980/81, a figure which would have been difficult to believe even five years ago.

For Product Safety Concerns and Information please contact our EU
representative GPSR@taylorandfrancis.com
Taylor & Francis Verlag GmbH, Kaufingerstraße 24, 80331 München, Germany

www.ingramcontent.com/pod-product-compliance
Lightning Source LLC
Chambersburg PA
CBHW052131300426
44116CB00010B/1857